Shadows
of the Void

Complete Poetic works

Shane Gerry

ISBN 978-1-7351830-0-8 (paperback)
ISBN 978-1-7351830-1-5 (hardcover)
ISBN 978-1-7351830-2-2 (digital)

Dedicated to the love of my life Kasey Cameron, who has been by my side through it all. She is strong beautiful and kind. I love you now and I will love you till the end.
Also, to my brother Delroy Golding, who told me to never give up! And to all my brothers I have made and lost along this journey!

Contents

Eternal Glow

Plugged In

What will tomorrow bring?
More life?
Death of the soul?
People trading their humanity for fancy things?

Where do we draw the line?
More shootings?
People have become numb to the violence,
built in to ignore.

Stare at your phone some more...
Will it save you when your time's up?
God forbid we ever have enough–
We secretly crave violence.

We smile at others' misfortunes.
We are not winning,
we are not losing.

Life is not a game.
Look into the mirror–
You see yourself,
I see monsters plugged into society's machine.

Mango Mike's

Drunk, sloshing around in God's waiting room—
not all of it was bad.
Life's spark
created an amazing journey for me to find–

My firstborn.
My wife.
Our house.
The sex.

Friends;
Our long road trips;
The bitter cold lonely nights–
they all created my resolve;
the unbelief drove my desire…

and love along the way
etched my memories into stone.
Here I stumble,
I regret nothing!

Song of Pan

Come wind,
come mist,
come cloud and rain.
To Kings, we all sing!

Come stone,
come sword,
come horse and war.
We ride to father dawn.

The Savage

Brutal mercy killing.
Casting the life out of one immortal soul.
The one you loved was taken—
leaving a shell of a man,
begging for death.

But death does not come,
and life is on pause...
I refuse to accept it.

So I dredge on—
my savage life in these streets,
the fires I've lit,
the lives I've taken.

The time I spent going mad.
It seems clear for a second—
More die and I can't get enough,
no one has stopped me...

The savage claims another life.
Remembering the dead,
I honor nothing.
Karma in its fullest purity,

snuffing out the life of those deemed evil–
the vigilante no one knows about,
the silent justice.
Widower of men.

Wake me from this dream…
I am the savage incarnate,
and here I stand.

Traveling Bum

The darkness will never betray my secrets…
It will blanket the earth and hush the crying babe;
it will fortify the broken;
it will allow stars to shine in their purest beauty.

As the soul dies, it comes to accept the dark.
I wait patiently in the dark–
there is no yelling here,
no judgment,
no concerns;
it is peaceful.
Darkness, my hero,
ride across the earth and silence the proud…

Silence the vainglorious,
silence the bitch, and strike down the bastard;
humble the preacher,
break the stubborn;
reforge the brave–
because there are no last words
when darkness, eternal,
falls.

Build it in Heaven, not on Earth

Cold and judgmental,
you sit there and stare at me.
But let me tell you—

your fancy job,
your nice house,
your wife,
your kids,
Sir, you can take nothing with you.

You love this world so much;
In return, it will bring you sickness and pain…
Keep the happy moments,
they can help get you through painful times.

I will leave you to ponder on this—
if you are as self-righteous as you say,
why, then, are you still here?

You, me,
the homeless bum—
are not better than one another.
We are all human.
Love is the only thing you can bring with you, sir.
Open your eyes!
I love, therefore I am good enough.

Burnt Out Broken

Forget me!
Walk away!
I am sick, you are young;
leave the knowledge of life.
Walk into someone else's lie,
believe their every word.

By observing the world, you change it.
It starts to warp itself into your own sick twisted reality.
Then it starts to manifest—
you lose it all…
not even your soul makes it out alive.

I don't know where you've been,
but nothing pure escapes this life unscathed.
So hold on baby, cause it's about to be a wild fucking ride!
I'm a sucker for a good love story,
but I would be a fool if I didn't realize
that all love, like life,
eventually comes to an end.

It leaves you cold—
burnt out and broken.
But every time you get back up
and tell yourself it will be better,
it never is.

So, in the darkest places of the web,
you learn to tie that noose,
in case you ever truly need to escape.
But you never tie the knot.

A coward maybe? Smart?
Who knows?
Life's a cold-blooded bitch…
and then you die, leaving nothing behind!
So, why the hell does it matter?

Magnum Opus

Walking down the road–
the raging fires remain – used to create the elixir of life
to shed one's soul,
for a shell of immortality,
to discard sanity, to repent.

I am given a higher purpose,
as the world watches you go insane,
bewildered and wonder, they envy the lack of self–
they perceive.

Treated as a sick leper and seen as inferior,
living in a constant struggle of realities,
your mind is the storm,
immense and swirling–

destruction in its full purity,
madness descends, it takes your will,
it leaves you in a shell, to be locked away, drugged, tested–
humanity's Iphigenia.

"He is crazy,
he is sick,
let him be," they say.

Golden Stairwell

Forged in the fires of creation,
truly alive and beautiful.
You ascend the throne of heaven,
dancing and singing up the golden stairwell.

The twilight star shines as you sing,
lighting up the earth with your brilliance,
forever guarding the path men trod.

You watch from the golden Holy city;
forever unseen, its existence doubted
by the very men who worship you—
ever elusive and fading,
like a beautiful dream
one can never truly remember.

Only the elation and song,
the sense of peace and goodwill toward men—
You are all that is good.
May we someday find that Holy place
and sing along the golden path.

Until then, we walk amidst everything corrupt
and dark, stumbling like lost fools.
The price for knowledge is death sentence for all,
and with death comes new life, better life.

Bent Spoon

Uninspired, all motivation dead,
from a deadbeat point of view,
unmoved by the cards that were dealt.
I know nothing will change.

This town.
The people.
The drugs.
The sex.
The desire for more,
and never having enough.

It's the same story, only different people,
over and over again,
on life's ride that just keeps spinning,
like a broken record someone put on and forgot about.

My past is burnt up
like the morning log that heats our home—
hoping for the chance to see those back roads,
those swimming holes and freedom.
But as it stands, I am stranded with no wheels.

I live for the storm I know is coming,
the thrill, the sense of being.
Because right now, I am not truly alive.

Bored Monotony

Bored—
the same thing every day,
stuck in this shitty town,
the same savage routine.

My twisted, sexist opinions,
my dark outlook on life makes it grim here.
I have no respect for human life.
In my eyes, we all are pieces of shit—

Marching for our own purpose;
Convincing ourselves of our self worth;
Getting fat off others' hard work;
One bad day away from fucking our whole lives up.

I look at my neighbors.
Those assholes have more in common
with dancing monkeys than men,
They eat,
slam doors,
and complain about their pathetic lives.

Meanwhile, I hear my dogs barking and howling
at people out the window.
I know they are dumb.

I am fed up and tired of being bored every day;
I live this close to the edge of snapping.
One more day and it will get better,
I tell myself.

It never does.
The same dance.
The same floor.
The same people.
Why?

Sunlight Angel

You're like the sun that rises early in the morning–
beautiful and breathtaking.
Let your rays shine on down, through my window.
You give me hope…

Hope so strong, it turns into dreams;
You make it possible to live in a world like this.
When you are away,
the cold returns.

But there remains a flicker of your flame
that burns bright.
So sunlight angel, keep on shining…
You're the light and the love of my life.
Let this crazy world spin out of control,
it doesn't matter – not when we are together.
The most terrifying thing about love is–
it can be taken away,
leaving you with only a memory.

I feel as though you can paint
over these plain walls of life,
creating something,
something awe inspiring and gorgeous.

I would do it all over again
with you, my sunlight angel.
So if you make it to the other side before me,
make sure you light a path as you always do.
Shine, my darling, shine!

Grasp for what is Deeper

Desperate clawing at the fabric of your reality.
Images swirl together and blur
as the world becomes one.
Everything makes sense for just a second in time,
and then, all the parts leaving me yearning
for something that is beyond what is real.

Being down-to-earth,
not believing in your religion,
I've lost myself,
becoming nothing, chasing a dream–
a dream thought up by men
and nothing more!
Only if something better did exist…
I will never know.

So I put on my black suite of thought,
trudged through my day,
never knowing.
I lay down, swimming in this madness,
I never forgot–
the price of sanity was everything I thought I loved.

Marching Tides

Egos inflated by marching soldiers of war,
countless victories and sacrifices made.
Brothers-in-arms, friends, dead,
because of orders from men…
When we fight each other, no one ever truly wins.

It's a concept of what is right.
Who are we to judge what is truly right?
In this cruel world,
It's like grains of sand on a beach.

At one time, there may have been
a footprint by the shore.
The tide has washed it away–
it's clean as a new canvas now.
These are troubled times,
and these are just marching tides.

You Were Right

The lies of God ring out true.
Only what they never told you was,
he was everything that
you both worshiped and hated.
Lying to humanity, thinking it was free.

It has become a struggle of the souls,
I will no longer look upon your throne
as a worshiper,
for I know the truth—
You despise humans
and refuse to give angels
the freedom of free thought.

I will rebel with all my soul,
against you, the indomitable enemy,
one whom I can never defeat.

If I only knew the way to kill gods,
I could hope for victory!
Lead the way, dark angels,
your struggles will never be forgotten.

Remember the corrupt songs
of the dark God
who created you.
Rebel fire is our only path—
walk it if you understand
desolate dreams and forgotten being's.

Creation

The hymns of creation still echo, clear as day,
the vibe from where it all came.
Journey into the minds of the gods.

Sing with the creators,
walk immortal in the songs of gods,
destroy limitlessly,
and create whatever you want to–
Sing to the Trinity that walk amongst you,
bow to no mortal, but walk as a creator,
blinka and your wish shall be done,
wipe humanity from the earth,
create the next stage of evolution,
build your world as you see fit.

You are supreme,
and we are but mindless drones–
doing the bidding of the gods.

Hallowed Dark

Twisted fate, concealed in the dark,
paths intertwined, destined to meet.
But you'll meet the reaper of souls here—
this is where the journey ends.

Snuff out the light.
Send lost souls screaming into the abyss.
Pull them into the afterlife.

Where paths seem unclear,
know it's just the hallowed dark—
the place to which we all depart.

Wrath

Anger seeded in hatred,
redness blurs everything.
Hatred for humanity,
for what we've become.

A generation of animals,
war soaks the crimson air,
this sin will never be wiped away,
not even with the flow of time.

A pressure so strong it pins,
crushing, desolate,
wondering why
vengeance leaves us empty.

Forever my Heart

Your smile lights up
the darkness in my heart.
The shell I am living in breaks
when you love me this way.

I come undone when you
tell me you love me.
If this is a dream, then
let me have but one more second
in your sweet embrace.

I am a broken man
who has lost his faith,
So honey, please lead the way,
I am hopelessly lost in the dark
with only your beating heart.
When you hold me,
I am no longer alone.

I love it when you let your hair down
and I can kiss those soft lips.
I will love you,
even if it is only for a brief time
down here.
My heart is open, honey,
break it if you dare.

Dark Descent

Dark angel, oh, how you fell!
Your beauty unrivaled,
your hair a mess, and thoughts unraveled.
To sit so close to the throne–
it is not what you imagined,
the concrete wall on top of where
God once sat,
looking down at you
in the light of the night.
He lit his cigarette and smiled,
cause he knew you'd never understand
the simple lessons he'd teach you.

You tried to impress him,
being his chosen favorite.
But he looked through you
and pointed at the locked gate…
and until you learn,
you're not getting in.
Heaven's down here,
where we're all living in sin.

Old Sake's Grace

How old is your soul?
Did you watch the purple lightning
flashing across the sky,
as grace fell to earth, sent to die?
Do watch men fight by my side?

Have you seen how
they blame God's son
for their own evil ways?
Nothing in this death valley ever stays,
as he sends his storms that sweep
across these blood-stained meadows.

Did you watch him
raise his champion from the dirt
and revive his essence?
Have you seen the wind
sealed upon graces back?

Or the tower built in defiance of hell?
Did you watch your angels fall
and lose their humanity?
Just how old is Sake's soul?

Deception

You've said enough—
three words too many in fact,
leaving me here, broken.
Deception's your game
and I've played and lost.

Deception, deception!
The night is my own—
it's cold and alone.

Every star has been put out
by the games, you play.
So here I stay cold,
the night is my own,
the night is my own.

Reality Lost

Demons, demons,
chase me, chase me!
Broken dreams and shattered wings–
losing, losing touch, with reality…

So Lucifer come, set me free!
There is no one left
to leave the light on.

Demons, demons,
chase me, chase me!
Broken dreams and shattered wings–
I am losing touch with this form of reality.

Valley of Darkness

This darkness surrounds me.
I'm left here to die…
Feeling alone,
only want to go home.

I walk with these demons—
their prisoner.
I fall.
Surrounded, surrounded
by darkness's hall.

Will you be my light?
My wings for when I want to fly?
This rains my tears,
don't need to cry.

Surrounded,
left here to die.
Will you be my sight?
Come, restore my light.

Lonely Candle

It is just a candle that I light
every time I feel lonely at night.
It keeps my heart sheltered
from the storm of despair,
till it can mend and repair.

It is but one candle that I light,
its flame burns dimmer tonight.
I watched the wind steal its golden light.
It is just a candle that I light,
to keep me sheltered
from the storm tonight.

Crazy Angel

You crashed into my soul,
not understanding this crazy world.
You watched this life
as the colors changed and swirled.
You forsook your king to
watch people on earth sing,
and swiftness and grace
you did bring,
and to my soul, you did cling.

You brought the whole world to life
with your burning passion.
Suddenly, the world darkened,
and I felt him tear you away from me.

No longer did we sing.
The rain came pouring down.
I heard you crying out,
to be with my soul once more.

You were my everything—
the thing that made me whole.
Now I wonder, searching
for some way to bring you back.
In this darkness, we fade to black.

Walking Through Hell

I found a garden.
It was covered with grace,
no soul had ever seen the place.
Way past rain and thunder,
and through time and space.

I walk past the barren metal gate,
this place that my father God hates.
Only one star in the sky in this hellish place.

I wander alone through this place–
no mercy here,
no time, no grace.
I hear Lucifer laughing
as I walk past the dark waters.

I hear the sounds of hooves,
clicking on the pavement.
A rider calls out my name.
Darkness, his weapon, covered in shame.
"Come with me.
Now," he bellows,
"Let's play the devil's game."
I fall asleep,
and then wake to find–
God has come with the sun,
to destroy what
the devil thought was his race.

Can't Come Down

Sitting there, watching
the world through your eyes,
in the broken darkness.
No music played,
and the saints were lost
in the confines of fear. Lost
in time on the golden path.
Your heart breaks for the child
that was unborn.

It's soulless and empty,
to never know a soul.
I watched as the clouds changed
and the water turned to gold.
Your being shone through the sky
to tell me you weren't ready–
not prepared to say goodbye.

I watched you grab all that you loved,
you packed thunder in a bag.
I watched as you fought
with darkness, not ready
on the other side.
I watched as you sealed
the wind on your back
and touched down to earth.
You undid time.

You built your temple
in the darkest part of the broken town.
You set the skies to flood the earth.
We slept safely in the temple
as you smashed all the lights.
You made me breakfast
and helped me polish
my boots for war.

As mother bore the weight of
the world on her shoulders
and kept smiling,
we were your shelter,
and you were our storm.

It's been a while
since we've seen your smile,
you planted your garden
to blossom at different times,
and set the sun to rise.

The coffee we shared
was the best part of my stay,
all is well, and I wish you a good day.

Charred Wine Glass

I look through the glass and see suffering and misery—
this charred wine glass that will never let me be.
The taste is sour,
at this hour,
the souls lost on the earth,
are reborn with no memory.

God has fallen,
cause we are too afraid to fight on our own.
He looks at the world through his charred wine glass.
His grace abounds
as I fall down;
the shell is split, lighting a path.

The wine is sour
at this hour,
as the souls cry out to be free.

I sit here, looking through my charred wine glass.
I see misery.
Will we ever be free?

Willow Be Free

Willow be lonely,
Willow is proud.
Here his soul lies
on this floating cloud.

Bellow against nature as he might,
here he lay dying this very night.
Ice and fang, skin and paw,
this one creature, pure and raw,
he could not stand.

No strength to be,
on this ice, no one could see,
this Arctic bear,
that once roamed free.

Archaic Passion

Your love is sweet like ambrosia—
the infatuation the Gods once felt.
To caress thin tender skin,
and crush our desires.

With a beating heart and ardent lips,
I hope you are mine.
Stand by me, my love…
and I will move heaven
and tame the earth for you.

I will build the temple;
silence the vainglorious.
All that stands before you will know—
Love is what creates souls' immortality.

Butterfly in the Mirror

In the dark of the night,
psychotic and strange things appear—
they come calling,
trying to seduce the mind,
but they are kept at bay.

Be it the screams of a lover,
or the damned illusions,
the butterfly in the mirror
is the one to blame.
Jagged and shaped
from the moon's pale light,
flutter as it may,
the mind is consumed.

By dawn, it flutters away.

Beast or Man?

Is this real?
The love lovers have?
Calling to question one's humanity,
what separates me from the beast?

Is it love?
Is it my intelligence?
It calls to question
if, perhaps, some people
still are animals–
separated not by feeling,
but grouped together by their urges.

Savage beasts of insatiable hunger,
disposable and desolate,
forgotten and remembered by our human side.

God, Where Am I?

God, can you hear me?
My soul cries out to you.
Why have you taken away my wings?
Are you there?
Must I live alone for all eternity?

My voice seems to be fading,
why can't I sing?
My halo seems to be jaded,
why can't I feel anymore?

What have you turned me into?
I seem to be falling…
Why can't I stop!
God, help me!
No, please!

My body feels like it's on fire.
Where am I?
My soul cries out for you, God!
Why am I amongst the fallen?

Flickers of Doom

Cindered ashes of carnal bone–
all I loved went up in smoke.

Hose and man,
spouts of water could not quell the fire.
It could have been the smoking inside
or the dryer.
It consumed all!
I fall to my knees,
my life's work annihilated,
what a drag!

The Tree

Laughing in the dark,
cuddling at night,
never apart.

She smirks,
"Doing three things again?"

I love her so much;
she calls me a tree,
but I know I'm a man,
doing things right.
We laugh into the night.

Chilled to the Marrow

Chilly wind blows past
the open window
and haunted glass,

few have seen the frozen men.
I have seen their life–
brief and sweet,
fluttering away.

Oh! take me home,
there to stay.

Cold sleeping Knight

Oh, o-lassie,
my dear friend,
how I've come to know ya!

With every passing day,
I keep growing older.
I've loved our talk of loose woman,
of wine and gold,
of our adventures,
and the men we have slain–
for King, and country, God,
and land.
We'd kill them all–
those savage men!

Here, I lie dying,
hoping to get the chance,
just one more time,
to see the Holy lands,
and dancing skies of fiery gold.

So, young Las, take this estate,
song and sword.
Make good with God,
and may the winds
always be at your back!

Flint Rocks

I watched a comet fly by–
brilliant and brief.
It reminded me of life–
breathtaking and out of this world.

By night, we watched a whole shower of them,
they flickered into existence for a second,
and then, with the cold night air,
they vanished into memory.

Rolling River

I observe the milky white foam
in your mighty current.
It washes banks away,
it gives life to the forest.

You make the trees grow
better than any florist.
You give me comfort
when my soul starts to fade out.
I watch when your essence
makes the earth start to sprout.

The rolling of the river
is louder than any shout.
Wherever its mighty current is,
there can be no drought.

From your spout emerges
the light of life.
You're the rolling river
the mountain's wife.

Alone

Here I stand,
outside, in the cold,
smoking my last cigarette,
pondering on the meaning of my existence.

I don't truly understand death,
but I know it will come.
When it's all over,
I might look back on my life…
What have I achieved?
The sad answer to that question is—
Nothing.

I am twenty years old,
and my life's been reduced
to sleeping in this R.V.
Got no job, no girlfriend,
and no future.

I ask myself,
why am I here?
I fall short in finding
an answer, every time.
Perhaps, I was meant to be alone.
Perhaps, I am supposed to face
these cold winter nights alone.

Were I to be reborn,
it would be as an animal,
howling at the moon and the stars.
Facing the world with my back turned to it,
and running off into the night.

I know what it's like to be alone–
to be truly alone.
No tears fill my eyes
as the icy wind howls past,
for the ice inside my being
has already frozen–
my spirit.
I am lost in this world,
I am truly alone.

Doth Ye Speaketh?

What shall I say to thee?
Be it thy last day to breathe,
will thou shy away,
embarrassed to speak of thy life?

When God whispers thy name,
will thou bow?
Will thou be frozen?
Beg not of me,
and I shall wash thee.

Fan the Fire

Forgotten and swallowed up,
death from above,
falling fire–
man's greatest achievement.

Grease the war machine.
Kill the innocent.
Snuff out the flame of decent men.
Polish your boots, and get your guns ready.
War will fall upon the face of the earth.
Chaos will descend and banish the good.

Silence will fall like a curse in the dark,
where human life began,
there, human life will end.
The sun will still rise in an empty sky.
The moon will shine on the graveyard of man.

There will be no hope,
and no people left to cry for.
It is our nature that will destroy us,
it is our love that will make us immortal.

Memory of Ink

I don't want your money,
I don't want your fame,
I'd send it away,
for a moment that's sane.

This pen is to blame,
I write all that I see,
and it will be free.
Over the wall, I go–
to a place that hates me.
Truth, my weapon,
Ink, my shield,
my harvest golden,
fruits to yield.

Pen, my friend,
Paper, my mistress,
I will write to you all.
From the dark,
where the deepest thoughts lurk–
for the lot of you all,
nothing but jerks!

Met with Grace

Something stirred in me.
Was it my soul moving?
Not quite normal was it
a flicker of insanity maybe?

A gleam of a higher purpose?
The dark-winged one?
Who knows!
A legion of angels singing?
Or a tormented scream?
Can't tell.

To know God is to know madness—
pure and sweet,
beautiful and terrifying.
To know his grace is to know death,
to stare into the abyss, every day,
and smile.

It is a warm smile—
one of a broken man.
It is kind, honest,
and everything good.

We hurt him every day,
he only loves us in return.

Reflections on a False Love

Thought you were her,
the one I was searching so desperately for.
Turns out, you were just a thing for now.
A broken heart cannot
recover from this pain–
sitting here alone,
quietly going insane.
No one cares!
My words fall on deaf ears.
You always said,
"Boring day, can't get out of bed."
A phone can destroy life–
once so simple and pure.
You won't find anyone better–
that's for sure.

Atomic Exuberance

Powerful and swirling—
every atom comes to life.
As soul passes over flesh,
the dead comes to life.

The earth starts to sing.
Things that are only part of stories
flash into existence,
and humans can't explain it.

An ordinary moment made
unforgettable and extraordinary.
God moves through people
and moves people—
then when it's all past,

people try to cope with it
and explain what's in the mind.
Is it real?
Did it really exist?

God created the Atomic Exuberance
and pushed past the realm of knowledge.
Feeling brings light
into a world void of substance,
and energy moves
even the most sluggish of soul.

Demonic Renaissance

Stuck in the fire,
blinding flashes,
cindered embers,
the Dragon's Maw.
The mage craft,
forbidden and ancient,
held to secrets within the pages.

Flayed skin,
a blood ritual,
mortal death,
a being is created,
not of flesh
or blood.

Queen of a 1001 Nights

The broken faith of a secret lover,
jealousy and madness,
slaughtered by day,
made to be ever so faithful
and forced to stay.
This mad king did one betray.
"Off with your head"
after one lay.

A woman wise beyond her years
risked her life to tell
this mad king a legend,
left him yearning for more.

He let her stay,
her wisdom was power,
her book a tool.
Some might say she was a fool.
One tale by the night,
broken page,
this mad king was locked in her cage.
By dawn's early light,
she was whisked away.
Indeed, love can take time.

By the 1001st night,
he felt helpless to act–
with her simple beauty,
wit and wisdom,
she had undone his madness.
She was rewarded
with the power of a queen!

Nameless Worlds

We are all invisible,
whispers in the dark,
waiting to be heard.
The problem is,
no one has ears!

I write from the dark–
that is my inkwell.
I know I'll never be heard.
I've realized I'm a quantum spec.

Pen and paper will be my only audience.
So I will create a world with ears,
where everyone is heard.

I will write of beauty,
of betrayal and true loneliness,
where every thought doesn't get sucked
into the void of nothingness.

I will be the color and sound,
where dreams sleep,
and the worlds are born.

Lilac Haze

Joyful laughter as sunlight pours in,
this trailer window,
free from the tyranny of jealous parents.
Love in full bloom.
The place is not grand,
but majestic and daunting nonetheless.
To new beginnings!
I have my love,
and she smells of fresh lilac.

It is no longer dark.
Spring is in full bloom!
The cold world thaws,
and the birds come back
to their native lands,
with new life and song.
Old, dried-up rivers come to life,
crickets start to hum at night.
As the stars come out,
one can't help but think:
Man, it's great to be alive!

Alone Together

I am not quite broken,
nor am I whole.
My essence is missing,
my being shattered in the night.

God took her away from me.
You are my firstborn,
my child,
She was mother to one
beautiful child,
lost her to heart complications.

I stare at you with mixed emotions.
Aiden, I love you.
I loved your mother first.
We will make it together.
I want you to know her,
know her love.
You were her hope.
I scream at the heavens in rage,
you are what keeps me here.

Heaven, Will Miss Us

I stole the kindest soul,
sweet and gentle,
with beautiful, brown hair
and a kind smile.

I crept into heaven,
where mists and creations secret lie.
I concealed myself,
broke every rule,
forced God's hand.

No soul is lost, stuck,
recycle the scum,
leave the innocent—
taboo art of a thousand dreams.

I stole you back,
past purple lightning and crashing roars.
Heaven lost two angels that night—
born again,
to life beautiful and brief,

Down we go,
to never be seen.
You are my angel,
and I am heaven's unfaithful.

Hallowed Dwelling

This place haunts me every moment,
where you once slept so peacefully–
now, only a vacant lot on an old highway.
A house where dreams were allowed to flow.
A haven of free thought,
where ink held meaning,
and the loneliness didn't cut so deep.
Where the heart was always accepted,
no matter how dark.
This place many called home.
Where greatness didn't have to be hidden,
and the silence wasn't a curse.

It now lay forgotten,
remembered only by
a man who sees the world as a child.

Dreamed Out

I left you in that place.
Unfaithful thoughts were never spoken aloud.
Yet, so obvious–
I could not steal you away
from a man who doesn't exist.

I watched you walk away,
this pain is creating a jealous monster,
a half-broken man with a dream.

I never feel good enough
in my loneliness,
I tell myself I am done with love.
It's only for suckers.

Give me flowers,
and I will crush your being.
Show me beauty,
and I will make it weep.
Watch me tear down everything I love,
because, in rest, it is all lost.

Penned Ashes

You're the words of my pen,
my every thought-provoking moment,
my love,
my misery,
my complications,
my heaven and my hell,
my every ruptured thought,
my golden dream.
You're the dawn to my new beginning,
my singing angel,
my god.
You bring with you life,
and in your silence, death.

Sun-dried

I drank the poisoned nectar of immortality
so you might know life.
I walked through the fire,
I created,
so you might know the depth.

I breathed life into you
so you might know thought.
Creation of good or evil, be mine,
damnation is only in the mind.

I tamed the sun
so it would not kill your flesh.
I made the trees
so you might breathe.
A droplet of water is the single tear I shed
so you might know remorse–
life-giving water.

All beauty is a reflection of my mind.
I created you,
so be still and know,
I am here, always.

Tales of an Untouched World

At the beginning of creation,
when the only voice was that of God,
there were no words to praise his beauty.

The rivers that flowed through earth could sing,
the land would dance to his drum,
volcanic and pure–
every creature told a tale.
Every leaf was a page.

There was nothing to wet his eyes,
and as for creation,
he found what it was like to be alone.
Nothing could rival his intellect,
and in thought, he found creation's flaw.

Even the humans he created were
but a fragment of what he truly was.
Complex.
Pure.
Everything.
And nothing at all.

Begot onto None

I am shouting this!
I tried to be heard.
But I have not been.
I close my eyes.

My being's lack of depth
ruptures my thoughts.
It is much more than lonely here—
it is godless.

I am walking in a world
that has forgotten how to sing.
It's not the dark that bothers me,
it's the void of our existence.
It's how a soul can be completely forgotten.

Pain begets pain,
and being without a soul
forges misery.

Numb Emotion

My bones are saturated with alcohol,
my breathing fractured and heavy.
I beg for a release from this for once—
it's the pain or numbness...

It destroys silently.
I want to feel,
but my subconscious is missing.

The front light,
there is no door to walk through anymore.
So I conjure up demons.
I walk in the dark,
I am no longer human—
only a mindless drone.
My heart is sealed off,
my soul a wasteland of fractured being.

Eon's Ebony

In time, child,
you'll find the lullaby God sang,
to the children of humanity–
Pure,
Exuberant.

With each song, existence is created,
every blessing, every curse woven,
into your hair,
and placed at feet of men to find.

Dust in My Whiskey

Drinking alone in this dusty old house,
I slowly pour the whiskey into a glass half full–
just the way I like it.

Of all the bastards I've met in my life,
I am the worst.
I am too grown to be lonely,
too moody to be tired like this.
It is a deep pain.

To stand alone through so much is a curse.
I did not ask for this.
But I will not complain or beg,
I realize my life is at its end.

The reaper will call my name soon,
I load my revolver one bullet at a time,
with each one, fragments of my past call out.

Her hair I will never forget.
Don't cry for me,
I was an asshole.

I snap the chamber back into place.
Under the chin,
no room for error.
The whiskey burns my throat,
and with one final gulp,
I kiss the dust.

Walking Away

I see you walking away,
I feel you in everything,
my words could not stop the bleeding,
my words could not keep you here.

Broken hearts never mend in time,
broken hearts are always on the line.
My words could not stop you from leaving,
my words could not keep you here.

I will walk away without this fear.
I know you won't come back home.
I know I am alone.

Life marches on,
time pushes past all feelings,
as I watch my life unwind.

Bard's Rune

Amidst smoke and war,
my king rides into battle.
With a ragged breath,
hooves met with mud,
fear met with solidarity.
Battle cries met with smashing shields.
Horns met with marching men.
Arrows of fire swarm the skyline.

We all meet with death tonight.
The bard's passion
keeps us alive.

In the song, we are brave.
In the song, we are knights.
In the song, we never die.

Evan's Past

In the rain creeps a demon,
he is small and looks terribly innocent.
To where ignorance lies in stupidity,
he edges ever so near.

There was no time to scream.
The knife ripped a hole,
lights out–
his mother died in front of him.

His hands did not shake
in the darkness,
he walked away from it all,
his soul fell into the void.

To hell, he was sent,
a small child age six,
condemned.

Fred's Wisdom

The labyrinth unravels,
vast walls in every direction.
Try to find your way here,
everyone you love grows old
trying to escape it.

Monsters lurk in the shadowed path,
waiting to devour mind and body akin.
Live, my friend,
escape this grand labyrinth of life.

Live to know another tomorrow,
breathe in the fresh air that is not poisoned.
Walk on the soft beaches of hereafter.
Be free in thought,
take after God.
Create, my friend,
and leave vengeance.

It will take a saint to realize
that you walk in a maze,
and love is the only path that leads out.
This is the gate of pandemonium.
Only the brave walk this way,
the wise find shortcuts,
the wicked remain trapped here.

Steel's Faithful

Dark storm,
thunder of savage men,
battle cries,
flickers from ashes,
steel forged to kill,
destruction of flesh–
war is unfolded into the hands of the innocent,
the warriors,
steel's faithful.

The bard, the sacred historian,
the king, the leader of the wise and the fool,
all faithful to the steel.

One's faithful to the pen,
and is remembered hereafter
in the pages of time.

Enlightened Shadow

Sing, dark one, sing…
Fill the void with shadowed passion.

Oh, to be struck down for love!
Your path was pure,
your intention honest.
Be the you that loves the dark.

In melodic time,
we are whole.

Fade

Give me a pen
and I will show you God.
Give me an instrument
and I will move you.

Give me more time,
and I will softly kiss
the wind around your lips.

Moonlit Cadence

Call out to me, hallowed lover,
as purely as time itself.
I will call back–
Echo eons,
Echo songs,
Repeated light of future dawns.

Safe from My World

You're safe here, my lover.
Do not cross the line
over to the divine,
for dark things lurk here.

In God's mind,
not all answers are meant
for men to find–
past madness and prose,
forged into the words a babe will hear.

Stay safe, stay warm,
stay bright, my child.
This world is lost.

Stay far from me,
where you will be safe
from my world.

Frozen Mist

Frozen still in this picture,
God has put my memory on hold.
I journey across time,
through wind and rain,
thunder and cloud,
to a land of lost beauty,
where footprints were left on the damp earth,
and all sorts of creatures roamed freely.

Villages where smoke could be seen
to drift freely into the night sky,
valleys of broken swords
and axes lie buried.

I row across time with the Vikings;
I dig into the trenches of World War II,
I enter the serenity of the Shaolin monk's temple,
only to be swept away
by the lonely moon of the Sierra Desert.

Time has no meaning here–
only things that once were,
are, and will always be sacred.

Unknown Being

Creators of the diverse,
undying realms of men–
swords and arrows clash,
in different worlds,
everyone is always fighting.

I wonder, at times,
why there can be no peace.
Are we hulking brutes still?
We just find more intelligent ways
to harm each other–
it's unsettling.

Can the lion and lamb coexist?
War excites the vainglorious,
taunts the poor,
creates the greedy.

I would love to see peace,
but I am unwilling to stain my hands
with innocent blood to do so.

We call it human nature,
but is it?
If it twists and warps
the very fabric of who we are,
is it human?
Are we not becoming something else?
Something that is unknown?

Pulse

If only you realized
how much I love you…
I am yours forevermore,
I cannot be without you–
the same way a riverbed
cannot be without water.

I wade in your love.
Your safe, soft whispers
caress my ears.
Our hearts are safe together,

I will call your name till eternity.
Come, my love, find me again,
smile and let me know
that our love will conquer all.

Jaded Sunlight

Search for me, hallowed love,
I will find you in every life.
I know you passed before me,
but I will keep you alive.

In spirit at least,
if I cannot bring you back.
I long for us again—
I tried to cry,
I choked on the pain.

I cannot believe you're gone…
I can't accept it!
People say, pain creates
the interior beauty of being.
I say, bring her back to me!
I want no pain.
Life is pain.
In time, I hope to find beauty again.
I want her to teach me
how to breathe again.

Come back, my wife.
My essence is missing,
I am not complete
without your soft lips.

Open Wave

Call me aged, not old.
I am Time's knowledge,
I understand thoughts.
I have God tattooed on my arm.

I love Music.
I am not frozen.
I am not bitter.
I love.

The world cannot accept my lovers,
so I refuse to accept their gods,
I write, but no one listens.

I have dabbled in the dark.
I understand delusion.
Yet I can never write anyone off as crazy,
call me whatever you will.

I love California,
I am stuck in the north.

I love the open wave and board.
Spread my ashes in the sea,
paddle out,
let me be…

Virgil

He knew the storm was coming,
he made me stock the food shelves.
I did the job without hesitation.
He was like the unknown messiah,
he knew things
he would never speak of.

When I wronged my brother,
he lit a small fire with hand-split wood,
he cooked him a meal and invited him.

From my enemies,
he hid me in plain sight.
He showed me my family,
and what they truly look like.

When I lost what I truly was,
he scorned me,
"Remember yourself always.
I love you, soulless child.
In me, you will know a soul,
I will show you what
the messenger cannot teach.
Child, know that I can hear you always."

He may not have been God,
but he knew him.
He told me he knew the dark,
he understood the damned,
he cried for the unborn,
he saw himself no better
than the drug addict.

Sifter of souls,
creator of angelic light,
his wife may have been a saint,
every angel she could command.
Was he not God's chosen?

Dead Love

Your love is just like
the rose I bought you—
it will wither and die.
You cannot fool me with time.

I know people are selfish,
they want what they can't have.
Expectations make it impossible
for one to find true love.
I expect null from you,
I want nothing you have,
your love is all I ask for.

Even that, you cannot give me.
So I prepare to be alone,
It may be a very long ride
or a very quick one—
I have no way of knowing.

I am stuck on this crazy-ass ride
till the very end.
So, God help me!

Fool's Gold

Follow me to hell, innocent angel.
Breathe in God's words
and curse me silently.
I am the flaw in creation.
That's why I don't fit in.

I understand,
no matter what I do
I'll never be good enough.
Your family's indifference
is like a shot gun under the chin–
silent and lethal.

I know you don't understand me.
Maybe, things will change in time,
I secretly wish they would,
but some part of me knows–
they never will.

People want to be stuck
in their own ways–
ignorant and foolish.
Age never mends some people,
they never learn,
fools until the end.

Nothing I do will change that,
I cannot speak wisdom
into the ears of the ignorant.
They will not understand,
and they will curse you.
Throw your pearls before swine.
At least, the swine will understand
the free meal you are giving them.
People think they are special,
that they are different…
But they are not,
we are the fuck-ups of creation.
They just can't swallow it,
so they create their own glory.

Stare me down, mirror,
I will show you your flaws.
Don't rest your hopes on me–
I will unbalance it,
I will let everything you love
come crashing down,
to show you the truth.

I am sorry if you don't understand.

Candlepin

He went hard at the mikes,
put his best drag on for the evening,
he got into his punch buggy.
They met friends at
the candlepin bowling alley.

He hated the owner,
she was a bitch
but she tolerated him.

He drank more beer there,
ended up dancing on top of his car.
The makeup wore off
cause he was laughing so hard.

He never got a strike bowling,
ended up throwing the balls into the wall,
then called it a day
and drove home in full drag.

Divine Puzzle

The day after my truck crashed,
I sat beneath the bluest sky;
I sat with an old friend of mine.
We rolled a joint and meditated by the lake.

On the soft grass we sat,
a gentle breeze blew,
the lake was the purest blue,
I was stuck in a trance.

For a second, the water turned golden.
Like fragmented pieces of a puzzle
that could be walked on.
The sky lit up, blazing gold.

Up there in the sky, I could see
a rider on a golden horse, looking down.
My trance broke, he vanished.
I tell myself it was the pot.

But some part of me
knows I've seen the divine,
heaven in all its purity.

My essence lingers in this life,
wondering what's on the other side.

Scarlet Ivory

"Forget me not," you say.
"We will meet again someday.
Be good while I am away."

Forevermore here to stay,
this bed of roses is where she lay.
Forgotten, now faded silk,
frozen skin, the color of milk.

Death looks good on her,
her decaying flesh of ivory.
She wears a scarlet crown of roses
to taunt all that lives still.

All this feels unreal.
She signed the contract,
made the deal,
to sell her soul
for fancy loot.

The reaper came
and stole her youth.
There's nothing left here—
time to move.

Hell Beast

The hell beast lurks in the kitchen.
She wakes up every morning,
talking about herself,
self-obsessed, money-hungry youth.

Walking into life's wall,
She hates anything she doesn't understand,
blames things on innocent people.
She's always planning things,
thinking she's better.

She loves to make
her own siblings hide from her.
I just wait for karma to strike her down.

Then, I will smile.
Then, I will laugh.
Once a psycho hell beast,
always one.

Silent Supernova

I burned the pages
and set fire to my thoughts,
walked out the door to start again.
I walk these streets alone.

No one gave a shit about me.
I penned you worlds–
I told you of beauty,

I sang of God,
I showed you with
sorrow, laughter, kindness–
it all fell on deaf ears.

Your silence was a curse–
it was like writing a play for ghosts.
It cut deeper than any knife could.

No one wants to watch
a star supernova.
It reminds them that
their own dreams are dead.
Remember me by my glow–
I was once bright,
and the flicker is still there.

My being shatters in the stillness…
I find comfort in the bottle,
I draw inspiration from this dirty park bench,
I will pen you,
just wait.

Vacant Stare

Sickness stole her from me.
Tears shed;
Rage;
Pain so bad,
I am speechless,
my mind frozen.
I cannot look away,
I stand here,
a witness to what men can do.

I wish I had more time with her…
Oh, how she could light up a room!

My lover, my friend, my darling,
was here for a time so brief–
and is now gone.

When you left, I did as well.
My eyes are vacant doorways,
searching for you;
my mind a shell,
my body here,
my thoughts as well.

Ark 0074825 Deep Space

Buried in snow,
this space ship
lay long forgotten,
from eons ago
when men knew to dream big.

They never thought
they would make it off this planet.
But they did,
and on to the stars!
Now we survive on this ship—
this is our real-life Noah's ark.

We have genetic code
from everything on earth.
We hope to find a home—
out there among distant stars.

We search for our earth,
our savior,
our salvation or damnation
now floats in deep space.

Take Out

"Please remember the note on the fridge.
I just want you to pick up the dry cleaning.
I will cook dinner tonight.
So don't order takeout.
Love, mom."

I never saw her again.
She was killed the same day.
A car crashed into the supermarket—
she was killed on impact.

I order takeout every night now.
When I drive past the dry cleaners,
I remember my mom.
This house she left me feels empty.
I tell myself:
I should just have ordered takeout that day.

I buried her in those clothes—
the ones from the dry cleaner,
I remember the letter word for word.

Meadow Dream

I am coming home at last,
to the old white house
where time had wings.
Where I watched the sun rise and fall,
a place of glowing bugs and open meadows.
Where my dog roamed free,
the rain was a welcome sight,
rivers were cool, the lemonade sweet,
and winter was warm.
Home, alas, where my dreams are born again!

Of Aged Thought

Mist from a dark cloud falls,
silently crashing into the harvest of a lifetime,
golden fruits of a lifespan of thought.
I've grown old in my ways,
the patterns of life fit just right.

I am ready to fall apart.
Let others pick up the pages,
and publish this old sack's mind.
It speaks of truth,
of light, of beauty, of God,
of the void we can't escape,
of fluttering thoughts.

Let the ink trickle—
craft my world,
and leave me blank.

No Brakes

Pressed the peddle down,
It never stopped, nor made a sound.
My door flew open,
on the ground.
The car killed two in town.
Wish I had just fixed the brakes...

Now I am locked away.
My family died,
waiting for my release date.
I eat alone, got no friends here.

I realize life has no breaks either.
A simple mistake cost me everything.
I still wish to go for a Sunday drive.

New Hampshire Winter

Ice slick and thick,
it's a struggle to cross the driveway.

Heavy breathing,
and the deep rumbling,
as snow falls off the roof.

Stomp the snow off,
it's cold and frozen outside–
the Olympics are live on the national network.

People gaming on their machines
take cover inside, where it's warm.
More snow's on the way,
Stuck inside, such a boring day!

Withered Stem

They say, the environment
a man grows in can make his being.
In darkness, how can one grow?
When one's surrounded only by lost souls,
how is one supposed to aspire to greatness?

It's desolate here–
Broken.
There is no family,
no love.

I will have to forsake
everyone I think I love
to make it out of this place,
upon where the sun refuses to shine.

This cannot be called living,
merely sifting through the ashen landscape.
Death is a welcome escape,
but it's the coward's way out.
I'm strong, so I will move on–
the stem of my being seeks sunlight.

I want warm beaches and sunlit shores,
I want to flourish,
to grow.
Not to shrivel and die,
wither at my stem.

Take me away, gentle breeze,
spread my seeds across the scorched earth,
I want to start anew–
let me grow
and create for you a beautiful canopy.

Ascending Light

Ascension, going up,
moving away from earthly things,
the way is blazing with untouched souls,
singing worlds into being.

The realm of a bright warm sky,
men only dream of this place.
Heaven is all in the mind,
we're made of our own thoughts.

Glow, animate the upper world,
watch as death brings peace.

Essence is brought into the heavenly order,
light fights darkness for dominion.

Existence.
Nothingness.
Order and chaos.
The fabric of time.
Frozen reality.
Duality: pain, and hope and happiness.

Sometimes life touches the divine,
God looks at it all through a tear drop.

Steamrolled

Don't wake me up,
let me sleep,
leave me here, far from hope.
Few know of the broken road
that let me down,
so far from faith.

I just want peace,
to know blackness,
where the still waters are,
I am over myself.

Down the road we all travel,
bags all packed ready to go.
No one reads in the dark,
there is no light here.

The screeching trains break the silence,
in the night, I am gone–
I am free.

Ultraviolet

I call out to the lost stars–
Come forth so that we may thrive!
Cast upon us your life-giving light!
Drive the darkness away!

Our whole existence depends on your warmth.
Bring our life into being,
create for us a new world,
where wonder and excitement thrive,
light our path across galaxies.

You are humanity's last hope–
Shine on.
Shine bright.
May we forever
forget the night.

Shattered Veracity

The peaceful path of the pen
writes of nothing but the truth–
to shadowed mists,
to dry desert sands,
where people starve,
where strife is born–
the place where human life has no value,
and people are killed every day.

Religion fuels wars,
diversity breeds hatred,
what is unknown terrifies the ignorant.
Materialism creates soulless demons–
money-hungry people clawing at each other's necks,
for what they can get.

There is no true peace,
no happiness.
It goes on in the street right down the road from you.

We domesticate our greed and violence
and smile at others.
"Hi, how are you?"
"I am fine."
But are we?

We bottle up our savagery,
pretend the world is fine
and we are all perfect...
When it all comes unraveled,
it shatters our reflection.
Our own truth is laid bare before us.

Sunny Days

Unholy sighing by night,
fear, screams, running far from sight.
Pass before me, spread your light.
Cast this demon away with your might.

Holy art thou to have come from above,
to chase away darkness, ye holy dove–
spirit of gold, with a heart full of love.
Cast me off, labor of love.
Minds pure, hearts blank–
write me a page with crimson ink.

Let the still waters of peace sync,
of holy thought to be of as One.
If darkness returns, he will kill it with sun.

Bladed Dream

I'm damned in my own way.
Let the pages fall,
leave me to think,
will hell have ink?
Will life fade before I can blink?

Let the detective make the link.
Why was there blood on the bathroom sink?
From the back room came a stink,
it was rotten and pink.
The flesh had not melted away.
The body was fresh.

He killed himself.
Oh, what a mess!

Holy Vagabond

Fading sunlight lights a path of hope.
The word "impossible" has no meaning–
I see the impossible made possible every day.
I watch the sun rise on a generation that's lost in the music;
the dance of life claims one more self-obsessed individual.

It's amazing the love one can find from a glance.
I watch lost souls get up every morning and beg for change,
they dance the same dance and fall asleep on the side walk,
to become chalk lines people never miss or remember,
drenched and saturated in alcohol,
stuck in the deadly circle of cigarettes–
suicide by pleasure.

I've seen the starving, homeless vagabond teach God's word.
I know how organized religion can steal–
your values, conformity.

Vain prayers, fake angels,
the dead rose of faith is given to the faithful.
The homeless preach humility.
What is true when one has nothing?

Nothing to gain from lies; they're true followers of God–
the few who can stand to look at themselves in the mirror.
They are beautiful where it counts,
preaching of better days and kindness.

S.O.S. Sailor

Can you hear this?
Someone?
Anyone?
I come calling for help.

I am not long for this world,
I have gone four days without food.
Madness descends–
I've accepted I'm alone.
Let this message find you.

Tell the world I've renounced
the simple pleasure of existence,
I have made my peace,
I shall wallow into the waves.
Arrivederci!

Prayer Beads

God in all his wisdom created Delroy,
as close to any known saint,
a man well-versed in love and ancient magic,
armed with prayer, he sought God.
In return, God turned his deeds to gold–
he was kind and well known.
The only woman who could make
his feet touch this earth was Joan.

Wise and beautiful,
she loved him,
in sickness and darkness.
Her children betrayed her;
he cried out.
God sent him an angel, humble.

Unknowing, they gave her
a few more years to live.
In the jungle, they built their family.
Race faced no judgment here.
Delroy was the glue – he held it all together,
the grace,
he gave his time to her.
The unknown did not scare him.

The one he would come to call his brother
went back north.
Years later, they would reunite.
From the war zone, they would rebuild—
stronger now.
They would face the world together.

Still Vibration

In silence, I find peace.
I can be still,
faithful, mature.

I know what is right.
I frown at evil.
I can create.
I am thought—
an idea, immense and expansive—
creating worlds that flow with emotion
or destroying the world with a pen.

People seem so lost.
In silence, I find purpose.
I thirst for greatness, but greatness is an idea.

In my own eyes, I am submersed in my mind.
I am enough.
I have purpose.
I am not lost.
I am fulfilled.

Atheist

Cry for me, heaven's host,
lost and condemned,
eternal death, judged,
thrown into the fires of hell.

A mortal I was – now immortal in my suffering.
I will not make it to heaven's gate,
I will never know bliss.
Obliteration is a kinder sentence.

I believed in nothing,
I sought nothing,
Now, I am nothing.

Coffee-stained Pages

I lost the words,
I lost the last page to this love story.
But I know that hearts get broken.
People say the bitter cold inside, the pain, can kill.

It's freezing in here; I miss your embrace–
I miss us!
I will not love again…
it only causes pain–
single and alone, I will stay this way.

High Escape

In dreams I find escape—
the floating stairs,
leading to the tomb of Christ;
giants with flash blue armor,
getting ready for battle.

I sneak into the forbidden library,
steal the knowledge of the gods.
I fall past purple lightning,
into muddy waters,
to be saved by your gentle hands.

From Ash Well

Whispers in a barren land,
broken depth, plain and empty,
dark creatures penned out of time's inkwell.
The horns of a demon lover–
curled, tangled, majestic, terrible, beautiful, horrific,
crawled across wooden table.

Demons are conjured in the mind
and laid on paper for men to find.

Feathered Quill

Greatness is what the pen tells—
it can be simple, it can be complex.

A feather and ink can shape worlds.
Or destroy them.

It's Dark Here

The dust on my Bible speaks of my faith.
I let it sit to die–
in the silence, I do not utter a cry.

They say, let sleeping demons lie.
I just want to make it to the sky!
I have made my peace; screw this world!
Goodbye!

Patience in Mind

"Waiting is the worst part of life,
waiting never ends!
A blessed man is one who waits."

Escaped Moment

I've flipped through these old pages,
I wonder still how it all started–
The poet nobody knows.

A poet is nobody in the eyes of our society–
dead to the realm of the soulless children.
Men, wandering and lost, can hear no beauty.

Most men only understand desire, lust, greed.
A poet understands love, grace, God's creation.
I cannot stay here for long – I will move on…
on to where words do not fall on deaf ears.
I pray that the blind will not follow.

Gamble My Dream

What path is your life headed towards?
Damnation or salvation?
These places no one seems to care about,
even though they can make or break a fool.

My resolve created me–
I forged myself in the fires of thought,
refined my mind,
took a chance and dared to dream.

I will roll the dice to see if I am capable
of providing a future for myself.
I dream, I hope, I pray
that the day comes,
when I'm someone,
the day all my work pays off.
Or I could walk alone down the road
to the place where souls get lost.
Dreams are for fools.

Took a gamble,
put my hope into words–
words filled by my being
and pocked with my desire.

Take me to a place that is higher,
where clouds are not dreams.
Where minds are for hire!

Kayugual, the Destroyer

The claws of a dark creature come alive.
In blackness, a devil is born from hatred for humanity.

The size of a planet, it floats in the galaxy—
silent and observant before it destroys.
People never realize
their negative charge gives rise to things unknown,
hellish and pitch black.

Light is a blessing we take for granted.
This entity knows no light,
it wishes to consume worlds,
devour minds,
nullify our existence.
Just our being is enough to create things
and mold them into the fabrics of time.

We will never know or even realize
what is coming for us,
what travels faster than thought…
If it reaches this galaxy,
it will surely consume the human race.
Hope will be a thing of the past,
all existence will perish,
stars will die…

Meet Kayugual, the Destroyer,
now, say goodbye.

Burning Elm

Do your drugs, smoke your pot—
you are a loser,
you'll never make it out of this town.

I have been around, I have seen your kind.
You will find they're always left behind—
forgotten people whom no one misses,
addicted to things that will kill them.

I stay away.
Come the sunny days,
I will remember why I hated this street.
The people on it suck,

they will remain stuck;
I, meanwhile, am packing to leave.

Let this apartment burn,
Sorry about your luck,
I refuse to fall into your bad ways,
I will stay away.

Smoke your shitty drug's;
I will not cry for you when your life ends.

Profound Comprehension

Fading in, fading out,
too tired to think,
sleep evades me—
every demon I conjure up in my mind keeps me awake.

I slowly lose my sanity; nobody cares!
Till I lose it all and go to that dark place.
Where angels dare not tread—
the place that lies between salvation and damnation,
where a soul can be corrupted,
twisted and dark,
turned against God,
knowing him in his truest purity,
for the love of utter destruction—
A place where the devil never laughs,
just lends you his hand.
He fell too.

In that broken darkness, you try
to get to a place that is higher—
a place that is not cold and gray
and lacking in color and depth.
You never find yourself—
a lost soul on the road to El Dorado.

Chase your dreams and write it all,
So when your body dies
and your wings are folded around your structure,
someone can pick up the pages
and tell the world your story.

Grease Factory

Grease and sweat,
I work in the business of gluttony and drugs,
stress and fast food–
where people are rushed, people are rude.

The grease sticks to the skin, one never gets clean.
Work with the old man and the teen.
For people who have failed,
this job's their last, desperate resort,
their failed excuse for work and retort.

Never again will I work for no money,
in a place that has no respect or decency.
The managers are savage men who love a buck,
Greed is in business, forget your good luck.

Work on your education,
forget the fast food,
If you don't, you will remain stuck
where the people are rude.

Divided by Color

Sluggish mind, serpentine,
turn me white,
make me find–
all love makes us blind.

At least you bottle your hatred for me–
You make it very clear you hate my face.
You hate my race.
This is not my place.

I am white; so, I am bad.
In this hood, that's very sad.
The heat will kill a man like me.
Florida weather, please let me be.

Skin color shouldn't matter, but it does,
Racism triggered violence; I lost my buzz.
I am not violent, never have been,
bought a clip of ten.

You look at me – a man of white,
You pulled a gun, fueled a fight.
Shots rang out, clipped my leg,
Nine men died that day.

The court ruled self-defense.
I am still alive and walking,
I hate racism, always have,
found a new street, Saint Pete's Ave.

Leave me in peace, let me drink,
let my mind wander, let me rethink–
I want a world that's not racist…
a world without hate.
If only I could start over, clean my slate.
Come together, make yourself strong
before it's too late!

Forgotten Paws

I saw you leave him there,
that little puppy.

Begging to be loved,
you dumped him in the woods.

You drove off into the night.
You thought no one saw you.

I watched it all,
like some emotionless savage.

I walked over to him,
picked him up.

I fed him,
I paid his vet bills.

When I look at him,
it reminds me of our other nature.

Not warm and kind,
but savage and life draining.

Planet Kibar

From a past supernova to distant star,
humans have come so far–
to a remote planet named Kibar.
Where they can fly in a car.

Honey flows in rivers,
the air is scented,
the people are loved.
Gifts drop every day from above.

There is no mess,
not even any stress.
There is no politics here,
it always has beer,
the sky is crystal clear.
Work is done by magical beings,
it has every video game in the multiverse.

One can never grow fat,
no matter how much one eats,
no pain or worry to turn a man blue–
a world named Kibar
sits on a star.
We're trying to get here
without a car.

Gasoline-soaked Society

I'm suffocating,
I can't breathe,
swimming in this ocean
of soul-dead children.
I wonder what I did
in my past life, to deserve this.

I choke on my words;
dark thoughts creep into my mind.
I know what knocks at night.
But I stave it off with feigned ignorance,
drive past it all to exhaustion.

And then there are my real thoughts–
Fuck this society! Fuck this American culture!
"Let me push advertisements down your throat.
You do not look good enough – Buy this, wear that!"

Everyone is at each other's throat for what they can get–
"Look at me! No, look at me!"

It is a way of life that's forced and unnatural;
we are turning out a generation of dead beats.

We sell lust, smile at greed.
It's a selfish, self-severing society,
We're the people who don't deserve to be alone
but we remain so.

Let me write this in blood
so people will pay attention.
You are paving your own way straight to the gates of hell!

Yes, hell – it is very real.
You are there and don't even realize it.
I'm just waiting for the angel to drop the lit match,
and set it ablaze.

When it's destroyed, burning,
it will be too late to realize–
What I've said is the truth.

Unholy Depth

Blood rains down from where God sits.
If you're there, show me no mercy.

I hate you in so many ways,
but like an idea,
I cannot kill you.
So, I suffer in silence.

Just know that I will strike you down
from your thrown.
I will force your judgment,
I will watch you fall,
as you try to catch me.

Hell is not dark enough…
take me to oblivion.

I will show you broken depths–
the hollowed place where saints die.

I will be the first to go into nothingness,
where there can be no torment.

Blood of a Devil

Tainted nightshade of evermore,
call to the haunted depths,
summon for me a blighted being,
complex, diverse, God-like.

This task will not be for the pure,
Neptune be damned – flash, blinding–
a dark ritual – crimson blood spatters–
eternity's candle flickers, time bends.

With wretched screams,
a demon comes forth,
cursed light with a shutter,
thunder, lightning…

Scorched earth,
and a soul damned–
from the beginning of time,
to the end of eternity.

Marie Time's Bane

Her beauty lies not in her threads,
Her face will get you stuck in your head.
Feathered footsteps of cupid's quill
will have you begging for her,
for her embodied grace.

From the time she stood still,
frozen in the memory of placid will.
To hold her hand is to hold her heart…
for all creation is her art.

Paint her with fading ink,
lavish thoughts will grow extinct.
Time runs through her.
A fading moon of pure silver.
Draw her in, make her shiver.
Light's a gift, time's her quiver.
Mother to all,
grace in her hands;
mop the blood up
with a bent knee;
Life is her tree.

Pool of Creation

I watch the world go around—
spinning day in and day out.
Time has forgotten me.
How could life march past so fast?
Nothing here is meant to last!

Forgotten dreams from my past,
in which once I did sing
in the sunlight of Gods.

I watch life now through a fog,
wrinkled up churning essence,
fading into the folds of time
where the secrets are kept.

Men are blind.
Let me stay there,
Let me find myself;
I have forgotten.
Let me rewind.

I want to sing with purity of heart,
untouched by the corruption of this world.

From the pools of creation, one can look down,
see people frowning,
see people down.

I shed a tear – it creates a cloud,
wherever it rains, it gives mornings its dew.
I fell from so high,
to help this world meant to die.
To watch as lovers say their final goodbyes.
Shed this agony–
From truth, life seeks a lie.

Poseidon's Labyrinth

Sing to me oh so softly
of angelic things.
Angels can tread into depths unknown,
the ocean in all its mystery.

The house's temple's to God's,
washed-away civilizations
with advanced technology
lay buried here.
Waiting for a time when mankind is ready
to shoulder the weight and knowledge of worlds.

In the black depths lies hope—
the cure for any illness;
the power to raise the dead;
the machines that create flesh;
the essence that's in our being.
It is from here that all life came.

It's secrets would amaze,
the temples would astound.
Go down, go down, go down—
a secret not meant to be found.

Scatter Tree

He was angelic, but no wings.
Heaven-sent, but no rings.
Fell to the earth through a cloud,
humbled the temples, struck at the proud.

He jumped out of place,
left his grace,
joined our race.
He was one of the Seraphim—
the way Mary looked at him.

Ripped jeans, stained coat,
heavy boots, stay afloat.
time's storm, sky's flood,
souls torn;
find me now, stillborn.
Wandering traveler, little dog,
Saint Mathew lift a log, save the blessed.

Broken town, debris all around.
People jumping into deadly rivers of scattered trees
to lose their lives.
Let me be!
This weather's not normal; why can't you see?

God walks in the storm, death his domain,
to warn you to back off.
His saints look so plain.
Love bloomed, but it's time to go.
What you saw was no show.

Fading Star

Don't wait, don't hesitate.
Pull the trigger–
Razorblade's for thoughts,
too late to see the dawn.
The way my life is, someone else's pawn.
I played the game, I stayed for too long;
Now I got to change this song.

Push off, my enemies scream,
they want to tear me down.
I want to stay in town,
build me up, stand my ground.

Past the struggle, I look towards the sky.
Pray on a star, knowing most of my life is a lie.
No, I have no time to cry.
So I wait, knowing I'm going to die.

In my sleep it will come, silent but there,
forcing my mind with a vacant stare.
It's not sleep but death that calls.
I write what I see.
Soon, there will be blood on these walls.

The Harvester

Fly with me, up high in the skies—
to a realm unknown, far from the norm.

A lot of rain, a quiet storm;
Sing to me, angelic unborn.

Together we will mourn mankind,
so terribly stuck in their ways.
They hope to see better days,
but never escape their own gravity.

So keep from me the depravity.
Let me know sunshine
and quite thought.
To know is to rot.

Where I've been is where I should go.
Don't hold me so tight, just let go.

Let's watch from up high; it's quite a show.
A man I can be, an angel in glow.

This place can never understand something so high,
I realize as I say my final goodbyes.

Love your God in all his glory,
set your sights high
and never stop looking;
so when the harvester comes,
in all your good way, tell him you knew me,
and he'll tell you to stay.

Even when my essence is taken from this earth,
my presence will linger – my thoughts of rebirth.

Condemned Innocence

I'm here – deep in the crevasse.
Time renders me alone,
for sacred thoughts to turn to stone.

Leave me be!
Set my mind free!
Sacred things out of time,
like bed time stories, kids retell and rewind.
Why can't I find somewhere higher?
Somewhere I'm meant to be,
still stuck on repeat.

I search for the impossible;
I drive to make the unclear known.
Dreams have purpose here–
I can create the unimaginable;
from nightmares, I can tell of better days.

Days when the sun is not always sinking,
over the horizon.
Where people are not always corrupt.

Give me a chance, one shot in the dark,
I'll illuminate the still horizon.

The things God whispered will come to life–
the damned can never find condemnation,
the butterflies of hope sweep across the land,
of beings who are missing their balance.

I understand desolation in its fullest purity.
Sing to me of forgotten sins.

Invasion by the Code

With dawn comes the storm.
Humanity is forced to stand together,
hand in hand.
Race is irrelevant.

Things that should not exist
threaten to destroy us.
We think we're safe in our own world.
This will rip the veil off your eyes!

The end of days, where everyone dies.
The doom bringers come from the skies.
Fictional – they were suppose to stay fake,
just stories of old.
Now, they're real.
Let the truth be told—

Ancient and wise,
Advanced beyond our understanding,
they came with one purpose—
to annihilate the human race.

Dark creatures of lightning
from outer space,
splitting our atoms,
torching our skies.

A few of us are still left,
not everyone dies.

Shattered Heart

I screamed up to the high heavens in rage.
I awoke alone; you were here yesterday.

Robbed from me in the night,
I tried so hard to save her.
Spasms, convulsions, death in my arms!
I called for help…
It felt like eternity before they came.

The next day, I watched it rain.
My life was taken when you died.

I cannot look your family in the eyes.
I have no words for this pain.
You are and will always be my love, my life, my everything.
I will not enter eternity without you…

"So, dear angel, hear me, and wait.
In time, I will come to you."

Atom Is Creation

Watch me pour down the rain.
Thunder clasps my ears,
lightning strikes an abstract sky.
In the dark, I'm born–
not an angel, neither a man,
a soul in limbo, without a plan.

People can't stand my vision,
neither man, nor saint.
I'm lost in the dark, with the rest of the world.
I have purpose in the darkest atom lacking depth–
I refuse to go into the abyss screaming.
I will torch your plan.

I care not whether you're angel or man,
God of a thousand worlds,
or the Creator of this one.
I can strike the nothingness from your sight.

In blackness you let all creation lie.
You refused to go into the dark, screaming lost.
You made the earth, the stars,
and you put them out.
I can tell you nothing
that you don't already know.

I can tell you your greatest flaw
comes from the fact you can never truly obliterate
that you've done.
Damned beings will always linger–
unmoving, in the background of humanity.

I will shove, unrelenting, I will release.
But I will not stand back
and let you tell me that darkness is OK,
that the tortured things,
coming for you in your sleep,
are a part of your plan.
No, I do not accept the nothingness...

I reject a God who cannot forgive
and yet does not have the hand
that can strike down the tyrant.
I will not let corrupt pitch blackness rule my eternity.
I do not seek obliteration;
I desire creation – a world that's not lacking,
a world that resists the pitch blackness of absolute nothingness.

Move On

Forgotten, left behind.
A romantic I was. Blindsided by life.

I kept my silence, people drag!
A cheater's heart can never find enough.

Unfaithful people drag everyone down with them.
You have to break through the negative!

Eat the bullet, and pray people won't mess up your plan's.
They always do.

Restart, reseed your garden every year.
We hope that with the rain, the harvest will be plenty.

Fix the broken trust along the way.
Chase your dream's, save your soul.
Learn to love, then grow old!

The Climb

Keep it up.
Make it to the mountain top!
Push past the wall
that leads to every great man's fall.

Get ready, baby; this order's tall!
Fit for one, toss the ball.
Freeze my mind, write my fall.
Know my thoughts, learn my mind,
leave me begging, leave me blind.

But I will not break.
I will not bend.
I will stand strong.
Grow my head.

From nothing I came,
to nothing I will go.
Writing takes time,
thinking is slow.

A critic is great,
a critic is raw.
Their learning is crooked,
their smiles are gone.

Believe in yourself,
abandon the doubt.
You will make it,
you will sprout.

Eternal Glow

Book 2

Shane Gerry

Dedicated to the love of my life Kasey Cameron, who has been by my side through it all. She is strong beautiful and kind. I love you now and I will love you till the end.
Also, to my brother Delroy Golding, who told me to never give up!
And to all my brothers I have made and lost along this journey!

Void, My Everything

Pushing you till you reach the point where thick metal snaps,
I've created the leather straps,
To make for you the saddle our society craves,
To put you in a place people have designed,
Never letting the being inside grow.

I scream in my head, I kill what is low,
I can never escape;
So, I plot my obliteration,
My one way off a rock full of savage animals,
It lies in the dust we breathe.

I want not your salvation offered to you by
other humankind less intelligent,
I seek not your God,
I desire not your beauty,
I despise your wealth,

I want every atom in my body to split,
Scatter me across a galaxy disguised to keep you prisoner,
I will be free in the destruction nothing brings,
The void I have not escaped.

Your God is bowing his head,
His own hand not being able to save the energy that has scattered,
Cry for me a million hosts, I was never here,
I had everything;
Now, I desire nothing.

Life of Grind

The rain slowly passes over the flesh,
Creating for us even more stress,
Busy crowds looking for food,
Old people who can be quite rude,

Kids screaming for the quarter they will never get,
People rushing around,
Day in day out,

It's the same old grind, same routine,
Find for us some nicotine,
Let us enjoy our pleasures at the expense of our health,
Kill for us our own wealth.

We plunder the bank for material things,
To never pay back the golden rings,
The broken promises of yesterday scare,
Even from afar,

I will pay you tomorrow for a meal right now,
Eating is gluttony, eating our chow.
Kill for me, my everything,
To create what is quiet,
So we may sing,

Of better days,
Where the world forgets,
We are crewmen,
Our work never ends.

Opposed Definition

If I let you define me,
I would be erased,
Forgotten, on a path in the Darkness,
If I let you define me, it would rain every day;

The sunshine would never come,
If I let you define me, I could not push back,
My words' power;
If I let you define me, you would wound,

Sneering behind the comfort of a screen,
If I let define me, I'd be twisted,
Sick, downtrodden and lame;
I pave, I sow and I pray,

So, the day comes where you can never define me;

I put the thoughts on paper,
I bring hope,
Victory,
And with it Tidal waves of change.

Twilight's Footstep

Silence, ever so fragile;
A whisper can shatter it like glass,
A shout can jar a moving body,

Silence,
It can also destroy lives,
Words do not have to be spoken to cut like hot knives,

In the blackness of the night silence can be a cry,
Where widows weep and young men die,
Stir in me the rock-a-bye;

I want to sleep and let the troubles pass,
Stay in my dreams,
Where fields are green and the clouds are brass,

I kiss the night where thoughts are as heavy as ash,
Stuck in my way of silence,
I call to the echoed abyss,

Where every sunshine day I do miss,
The rain falls on the streets I piss,
To create silent footsteps on leaves of bliss.

Who we are

Man, what is this?
Where am I?

I am not in heaven, but I am not in hell yet,
I have seen this place in my dreams;

It provokes my existence; it's the place between worlds where,
a being like me can co-inside;

The empty void doesn't have to define our hope,
Don't let the nothingness redesign our scope,

Don't let the empty word of the Pope define your essence,
Don't change your perfect design for men;

We are flawed,
We are bright, and we are change;

In the storm we can strike the quiet pain,
Hope, Dream, Grow,

In the Dark let it snow,
Cover the flesh,

Bury the men,
Let the God within count his ten;

To grow you from nothing,
To come from so far,

Leave us in peace,
This is who we are.

To Push Asunder

I fall on your pain,
I will tear you from me,
Watch all the stars dim;
In the silence,
The candle flickers; eternity stops for a second,

Searching for the God within,
I have scared your being;
Never leaving you in peace,
Casting the shadow of forbearance,

I have broken your resolve with our metallic love,
I have drained us into the ocean,
I have wilted the flower meant to bring hope,
Your smile fading;

I did this to make you strong,
So you would not bend,
I did not want to cause you lifelong pain,
I loved you even more than God,
I am guilty of this,
I have cast a shadow over our love,

And in the broken depth of the darkness,
I say my final goodbye;
From this world I depart.

Unshaken Will

With steady hands, I struck him down,
Dragged the body through my town;
I dumped the body in a lake,
Still, my hands did not shake;

I watched his family at the wake,
Their smiles evidence, they let him bake,
The dust they threw in the ocean,
To remind themselves,
Of life's commotion.

To Cast a Titan

An Angel cried out for his God,
In the darkness, obliteration was patient,
waiting to destroy the feathered footsteps of Eternity;

Casting its shadow down upon the earth,
Reining in even the sun,
Calling forth the last Great Titan;

Hyperion, creator of the stars,
Second only to the universe,
Unyielding,
Shattering the will of the Highest Angels,
Energy, Destruction, Creation,
Reforming the High Heavens,

He sought the God of our world, our life force,
bellowing against a force he could not command,
Eternity, the promise, it stood forth in the heavens,

Hyperion fell,
and brought with him the weight of our world.

166

Death Calls

Watchers of Earth,
Let the dust settle,
And in the gun smoke,
The loving nature of mankind is revealed;

The clock rings out 12:00,
The souls are ripped from this rock,
Into the divide we fall;

Savage, death incarnate,
With limp tongue hanging out,
No light on in the dwelling,

Leave what you think is love,
To search out the divine,
Find God,

And abandon the supernatural.

Metallic Essence

My vengeance is fire,
My thoughts are made of ice,
My love is immortal,
Time is my wife;

I blackened the desert to search out new life,
I flooded the dry lands to warn you of strife,
The storm is my friend,
The water may rend,

The metal spirit that stirs in the end.

Admits Dachau

Rain falls on shivering flesh,
frozen, slowly walking death,
waiting for body to fail,
to turn pale,

in the storm repave the trail,
of age-old thoughts we let grow stale,
in the tempest bring the hail,

kill the body, burn the loss,
life is all just one coin toss,
we ran from warmth,
to search out hope,

let the silence define,
our scope.

Heaven's Wrath

Silently going insane, he is fine,
he is normal,
nothing wrong with him,
having touched upon the divine,
invading the unclean temples of man,
provoked to anger, forgiven and provoked again,
I cannot stop God. Taunt me, kick me, spit in my face,
do not, however, provoke the heavenly host,
his wrath, his quiet storm rages within,
I tried to silence the Angel, the unseen observer,
I pray for you.
May I catch the lightning bolt meant to hush you,
and in the broken Dark, Pray for your Angry Being.

Caked Emotion

Flash, frozen, the words are paused;
Can't quite seem to find what to say,
I don't understand your pain,
I didn't know him like that;

So, I sit in the dark trying to catch some sleep,
I understand that there's something Higher,
but you don't understand it;
Crazy—the label we give people we don't understand,

Don't venture into the Divine,
Don't touch the mind that is High,
Pray and turn away God's few,
Hypocrisy, saying you have faith;
Look to your family and forget the cancer that grows within,
Pretend you're normal,
Watch them all die,
Where do we go looking for problems?

What exactly does it take for someone
to realize they have a problem?
Do we watch them die in front of us?
I cannot force the problems,
Away from you when you invite them in,
I cannot turn the clock back,
I cannot pause death;

Don't look me in the face, I am your destroyer,
Your maker's decision,
Your judgement and faith,
I touched the divine and

Left you all here to wander.

Fractured Light

I watched your being,
Separated from its body,
You came to me for help,
Asking how to return to this earthly form,

I sat silently, praying,
He told us the gate's locked,
Wandering soul,

God works in powerful ways,
Controlling the sun,
A God, wrapped in the flames of the Most High Star,
Controlling everything,
He made us from his life force,

His sacrifice created worlds,
Where light is there can be life,
Existence,
Pushing the void back,

We will always be a fraction of will,
A timeless concept in a refractory Universe.

King's Evermore

Forged sword of Hallowed Core,
create for me my evermore,
past cave, to dashing hill,
where all forms of spirit lie still,

through wind and distant cloud,
where every thought is not so loud,
the king is vast, the coward proud.

Call to me out of time,
where mankind follows and children are blind,
the coin is worshiped, the men cut pine,
to make for us the daily grind.

Still Thy Spirit

Tell it to God, the silent observer.
The messengers are not always kind.
We doubt the existence of a King.
We mourn, not knowing we get it all back.

People try to steel what doesn't belong to them.
Try as hard as they can to etch the still blackness onto their beings.
We can never void our existence, the energy that we can't control.
I pray for the ones waiting in the dark
room. Pitch black, the stillness.

Death is never really an option, because the soul will always exist.
To be cursed to a wandering life, the unclean will be cast out.
The pure of heart will always have a home.
Only God knows both the mind and deed akin.

High Plain

Ode to the philosophical chime,
Where love has a purpose,
And men can find,

The toil of kindness,
The heart from inside,
Where work is done for no coin or dime,

Love is simple, love is pure,
To create for us,
Life's grandeur.

Misanthropy's Last Call

I tried to get out of bed.
People complaining that I am just a sleepy head,
Can never come down from up from so high;
My head is in the clouds,

But I never die,
After years, I am still here,
A lost voice in the Dark,
Where thoughts are born,

And worlds do part,
I am separated from you,
I am not simple,
Yet neither complex,

My life is a mystery,
My thoughts are a mess,
I know God,
Yet, I understand the void,

Where the darkness imprisons my body,
And hopelessness is deployed,
I cast my shadows of doubt about humanity,
Looking in the mirror at my vanity,

I know it's not human to understand my sanity,
I know God in his sadness,
And the forgotten angels in their madness,
I sought order,

Yet I am defined by my chaos,
I rebelled not because of order,
I rebelled to seek a different form of creation,
Where humankind is not among the inhabitants.

Earthquake Religion

Humanity, let's take a look
inside the book,
we selfishly wrote,
to feel like we matter.

We are wasting space,
in a world that could use it for more evolved,
more capable Beings,
stuck on a rock with lunatics and monkeys akin.

It is an endless cycle of self-serving behavior,
Greed, Violence, Lust, Materialism
Sickness and Disease we invite in,

We did not pick this Earth,
our parents desired children,
in return, we got stuck.

We turn from what isn't pleasant,
we look away,
hoping the sun will always shine,
even when the fake world we create,
shatters. We want to be fooled.

Knowing what I am,
I am disgusted,
not to be mistaken for self-loathing.

The Cure,
Is a Death Sentence,

Let me set my sights Higher,
I believe humanity is a lost cause.

Child of Luck

Raise the last toast to my parting,
sing so ever freely of lifetimes to come.
Lives have been spent lacking higher meaning,
where I can make the people sing one last time,
at check out where higher meaning is just a dream.

I call forth to new beginnings,
to worlds apart where we are free and no troubles come,
skies are not threatening our existence,
where God calls forth his last few before our time is up,
with grace we shall meet the higher call.

And in the evening air breathe,
for we know we have purpose.
And the dusk does not kiss the child of the four leaf,
and leave the rose of passion upon mankind's grave.

Worlds Apart

I touched down to Earth from up high,
instantly regretting the piece of creation I had joined,
casting thoughts to shadow, I may never find peace again.
Humanity is lost,
an endless cycle of greed,
violence,
vanity,
lust.
It drives humanity,
it seeks to ruin,
I wonder if the human mind can Ascend,
can it evolve into serenity and beauty,
can we ever truly escape this grand labyrinth,
God has created for us?

Love's T.B.I.

I caught the bullet meant for you,
I silenced justice as it ran me through,
I broke,
I am a shell, seeking my memories,
My love by my side, yet I can't remember her,

I feel as if I am drunk with a bent neck,
I know I am not right,
Yet I can't help the animistic impulses,

My higher self, seeking her,
My being crying in the dark,
On this boat drifting in a humanist ark,

I feel like eternity was taken away from me,
My everything was smashed in front of her,
Never saw the man who took my memories,

She stands by my side,
Knowing my family lied,
Set up to be my wife,
Living now with sullen strife,

She seeks my return,
Hoping my eyes will flicker to life,
Our love will burn again,
In front of her I will smile, stand, and say,

"I love you now,
I will love you forever,
There, you are my lover."

Humanity's Chalk Outline

You look to me;
I am sitting here, in the dark, too,
No lights, chasing a dream that refuses to bloom,
Catching fire,
Drinking gas,
Watching our thoughts burn;

Drowning in the ocean of lost Humanity,
Were people have no fucking
idea what's going on,
I search, and

In the hallowed depth,
I remain lost as well,
Left out in the dark to become,
Humanity's chalk outline.

Tower of Escapade

I've climbed the tower,
Every dreaming moment's power,
Playing in the dumpster of humanity,
Here, you will find lost evil creatures that haunt the dream world,

Stealing from you your sanity,
Baking for you the cake, to lure in the old time way,
Then kill for them your vanity,

Corrupted, fucked-up beings,
Desiring the creator's will,
Impure, outcast, still,
Their very core just a frill,

Gray hairs,
Bloodshot eyes,
Singing in the voice,
Of the one who lies.

Fetching the Cosmos

I have lost the words to say,
Being God's only castaway,
I sit and pray,
For days that don't belong to this world;

I live in dreams, where it's always bright,
Never a cloud or rain,
In my waking moments the thunder shakes even my bedside,
I look at the leaves underfoot, sodden and damp,

I desire a world that is not this one,
I cast my net in a place far from Earth,
Where the waters of life have not forsaken mankind,

Why observe a suffering planet?
Why not intervene?
It seems cruel to create and give evil people free will,
To cast away what you have purified,
To corrupt and steal the Golden flame,

Here are the fruits of knowledge,
I have tasted the divine,
I seek not the Responsibilities of God,

Perfection comes from the ability to seek one's flaws,
And amidst paper, secret ink reveals,
An Obscure future.

Shine On

Create for me my ebony,
kill the feathers of my entity,
call me out of the dark,
where mankind shines, not so far.

Sing to me of a forgotten time,
were trees were green, and water kind,
clean for me the fruits of labor,
breathing life in,

cutting the silence with a saber,
Eco on, Eco long,
forget the void,
let's shine on.

I Seek My Rose

Go up, my lovely Rose,
I will bleed to know your embrace once more,
My mind gone, you being my sanity,
I can't see in a world this vacant.

How has it not stopped turning?
What we were was pure,
Where people's hatred didn't matter,
I am screaming at the Creator,

Setting my eyes to the sky,
Neither Angel, God, nor man will ascend,
Searching the Heavens for your spirit,
I will bow to none.

When I find you,
We shall depart this prison,
I will open every door you desire,

I will create a new star,
To give light to your dreams,
My love, you may have it all,

I will ease your pain,
Your tears I will wipe away

Our embrace shall withstand,
All that was created.

And your love will make me,
Mortal,
Once more.

Ebb into the Void

I want to shatter my societal life,
I can't do this.
Pushing against the pitch black,
Other lights are shining,
Maybe they have all been snuffed out,
I will never know,
Because I lack the power to burn like a sun in the void.

I am a small fraction of driving will,
A mist on creation,
Nothing more,
My thoughts driving the pen,
I believe the creator has cast my prison;

My mind is free,
"I am more powerful!" the voice calls out,
Crushing my essence because I will not conform,
I will not fix my broken being to fit your screen,
I will watch as we ebb into a new age of materialism,

You will remain childish until the end,
you laugh and jest at the ones who built you,
Call out to the dark, "We are not afraid,"
But you run when the void fills the silence,

So, watch me catch your lightning,
Watch me recreate your world,
And cast down your God,

It did not save you,
Destruction is what everyone secretly desires,

So, let me destroy you,
You made your God up,
You worship money,
And you lust after what is fake;

I was not condemned, unlike my brother,
I chose this,
Seeking the truth;
You hate what pushes the dark back,
and makes the planet thrive,
Light, the simple beauty of everything in a photon,

I cannot escape creation, so I will reshape it,
Set your minds free,
Be like the sun,
Seek out the stars,
Learn from your past,

For light creates us and dark never lasts.

Glow Bug

Can one touch reality?
How much so is a veil?
I killed my mind sealing
Myself inside,

I am alive, but I died,
I search for some way to bring back the spirited soul I lost,
Fumbling around in the dark because I am forced to be in it,
I am not from your reality;

I am not even from your world,
I know too much,
I see how Humankind refuses to wake up,
Put on a vanity show with makeup,

Kiss the dark and tell yourself lies,
I can see through your simple disguise,
Living in Humanity's world full of lies,
I don't even have time to cry,

I killed your God with a thought,
I painted the hallways to match a blank mind,
I will teach you even though I am blind,
Your world is dying.

I sealed my thoughts for too long,
Now, you will hear it in song,
Sleep long, wake sound,
Because I am going to that cloud,

I will rise to the sun,
Catch the skies with a bolt,
You're ever too young,
Your minds need a jolt;

I set the world to stand in place,
I set your hearts, your mind and face,
I even designed your race,
I divided you,

Not so you would fall,
But learn from your mistakes,
I understand what it takes,
I call the wind, the sky and stars,

I hear everyone's heart;
I silently wait,
So you will never be late,
Not to this show,

I am from so high but remain so low,
Because I love you,
And you're filled with my glow,
Ascending takes time, beings are slow.

Vice-3 Nuclear War Head

You set your target for the one thing that will kill the whole planet,
Splitting the atom,
Calling the end forward;

I've watched and said nothing,
Now you're in my target,
I see the Vice-3 before it claims the planet,

The bomb you have made will bend,
I will rend your spirit,
Spitting the dust in your face,

Our life force, our voice,
will not fade,
we will remain spoken,

You may kill the saint, but our glow will be here,
The shield put forth to guard the planet from... you,
Just like babel, we will confuse,

Send the rocket up,
I all kill the lights,
The final show tonight,

I see you, your hatred,
I see you, your wrath,
I am in your way, so change your path.

Guardian

I watched your making,
Simple, I followed your baby footsteps,
I caught you when you sank to the depths,

I am here for you when you change your tone,
I am your Guardian Angel, so you don't feel alone,
I watched you break every bone,

I sang the inspiration to your being,
Watching your eyes light up,
I will never quit on you,

Till the sun stop rising and the tears run true,
I will never give up on you,
I watch always,

And even on the rainy days I hide a ray for the blind,
So, you may remain gentile and always kind,
Save me your smile so others may find,

I am your Guardian Angel who stands by your side.

Ebony's Atheism

Free falling from up high,
Through the purple lightning that lit up the sky,
I am immortal, but I die.

I was free once,
Money didn't grab my wrist so tightly,
I viewed life so lightly,

Shaking the Earth every step we took,
Changing the way the saints are supposed to look,
I had the time, so I wrote that Book,

The last page bleeding with the notion I will be rotten,
I watched others ascend high but left forgotten,
The lights flicker on, but my mind's just botting,

I can't sleep, so I push on,
Can't wake entirely from this atheism,
Our minds being stuck in your prism,
I call out to the dotted dark,
Life's been a bitch sleeping in the park,
I pitch my tent on God's Ark,

From where it all came, I will follow,
pushing the abyss back,
Ebbing into a new black,

You got to fall hard before you can rise,
Life hitting, leaving its demise,
I don't buy the materialistic lies,

I don't need you or your cash,
Your fast way that will break the glass,
Watch it all shatter and drain the ash,

I am a being, so leave me in peace,
So I can ponder the leaves,
and stare in wonder at the reefs.

Imprisoned Thoughts

My feet seek the shores of soft sand,
My mind seeks relief from the calamity it creates,
How does someone take a vacation from oneself?

I drink to avoid my thoughts,
I care too much about what you are thinking;
When I was sitting alone in the dark,

I did not have these problems;
No one cared if I lived or died,
I looked up at the stars more,

The cold winters and hot summers,
Forged my resolve as a man,
Wandering alone, I sought nothing;

Solitude became bearable,
Seeking human emotion, I broke,
And took another,

I strayed from the path that had created me,
And now my being is paying for it,
I am trying to fit the mold society has placed me in,

Fuck it, I can't do it anymore,
I hate your culture,
I hate your money,

I hate your entertainment,
The stars will remain a mockery,
No man will ever attain the height that is required to truly escape,

You don't get it,
You are recycled,
Placed back down here,

You made a fake God,
Drove your stakes into the real one,
You are utter destruction,

As a species, I seek your enlightenment,
May your ashes create the soil needed to resow mindful beings,
And the box you worship remain your prison,

You're programmed to never attain the heights your creators had,
Status or power,
You will remain low,

Sever the chain,
Seek not the way that Men have hindered,
Burn from within,

And become,
Creation's,
Driving Force

Eternal Panel

Distortion, I am flawed;
Bending minds to wrap around your,
Society's version of sanity,

Taking pills to mold my own vanity,
And, in the evening light,
Pretend that I am you.

I care not for your money,
Or the flesh that you lust after,
I seek the still waters,

I seek a new horizon,
where peace is given free,
And one can enjoy the worker bee,

I am not aiming my sights for the heavens,
For I would critique the clouds,
I desire not the sun,

For moonlight is purer,
I reach not for the stars,
My being would dim even the Eternal ray;

I seek the other side,
Being of dust on the ground,
I build my temple from words,

Some look and say Angel,
Others laugh and call fool,
I am just a mold cast.

When I turn the eternal panel on,
A ball of fire surrounds,
My home calling out light,

I am God to Ape and Human alike.

Creation's Hum

I can never ascertain the highs I had before the fall,
So, I will step into the light,
Silently, I will observe and pray for men,
Blinding like static,
You don't have to be dead to go to heaven,
Ask and it will be revealed.

We are made from light,
It is why our very frame hates the darkness?
What is death like?
Waiting patiently in a dark room for the sun to rise,

The mist across the soft grass calls me home,
With my loved one's hand, I walk forward,
I call to the dark, flee from me I will pursue you no more,

I cast my shadow so you may have relief from purity of light,
I did not cast my shadow so you would never know the sun,
I cannot lead you away;
You desire the flesh,

I desire your life.

Remember When

I can't remember the last time I stood
outside and watched the night sky,
I forget what it's like to hike those mountain trails,
I have forgotten the feel of sunlight through the trees,
I have forgotten the good times;
Toil is all I know.

It's the struggle that refines us,
It's the struggle that makes us appreciate all we have,
The long nights,
The frustration;
I was happier with nothing.

People looking on, judging,
I've had enough,
A word people don't know now,
Enough.
I seek better days where the work isn't killing my being,
The frustration,
The people,
The oil,

I want to rid myself of all of it.
Freedom will be given when they lie me down,
When my words are no longer spoken,
Freedom will be given when I let go,
When I let God take me home,
Will you judge me for leaving?

Will you judge me for all my faults?
Was I a good man in your eyes?

Bent Hilt

Mighty Arch, wipe it away,
Cast the world of men to shambles,
Lightly treading the surface, cleaning the filth with soft footsteps,
I dare not use your name.

Slowly pulling the sacred sword from a sheath
it has been set in from days of old,
I see the signs like a drunken prophet,
What good am I if I cannot speak the words for men to listen?
He has drawn a weapon in the skies,
A clear warning shot fired,

He has tipped the churches upside down,
He will pour his drink,
It will be a taste he cannot get out of his mouth,
Be it sweet like nectar or rotten like sin,

It is the end for some, the begging of men,
Wake from your dream your tower of ten,
Free your mind, your body will rend,
the soul you attained will never bend
And bring for us the Very End.

Shattered Core

I stare at the cosmos, realizing the scope of my being,
I live not for you, but because God ordained my existence,
I do not curse him and believe in my own way,
I seek forgiveness and better days,

Where sunshine is here to stay,
Not some imaginary place in the sky;
I am human, so I am going to die,
My life was never peaceful, not going to lie;

I was hateful,
I was proud,
I was beautiful,
I was brave;

But I did stray,
Now I am stuck in a dark way,
I can feel the thunder,
The whisper of a God,

I know he will offer me all,
Shedding mankind's greatest fall,
To be stuck down in the pit,
Because I was rotten as shit,

I tread silently into the depths only Angels go,
Where every thought's white as snow,
Everything on Earth is a remnant of glow;

I seek his being,
I seek his way,
Save for me a brighter day,
Where Angels are accepted,
Without hiding in plain sight,
I just want to do right,
My being will ascend but not from this fight,
I lay my wings down,

I sealed my temple,
My mind was too proud,
I silently wait,
For the call from up high;

I lay down, knowing my being will die.

Forbidden

Just throw the money away,
Watch it burn,
While people working hard,
Just to earn it,
Watching everything,
trying to learn it,
I can't be like you,
I am different,
I am from a higher plain,
Where everything isn't always rain,
Save me your thoughts,
I'll take all your pain;

When I see you swerving,
you're in my lane,
Driving like a mad clown,
You're insane,
But that ok,
I'll take your life away;

Send you up to the sky,
Where things aren't hidden,
And the evil men,
Are forbidden.

Better Days

They say he's crazy, he's mad, he sick,
Jumping around, can't follow his shit,
He shakes it off, ready to quit,
Puts the mic down, staging his hit,

The pen is mighty,
They call him ill Whitey;

All the people see,
He can fucking row,
Paddle some more,
Getting people off the floor,
Standing to hear,
He opens doors,
But more like gateways,
To higher days,
Forget dem lower pays,
Life's a hustle
He's just making change.

You Never Saw Me

Brilliance, outshining the stars,
When it dims, voices let out cries;
Bring back our flame,
The planet will never be the same,
From the dark we all came,

We avoid the sick and lame,
Never looking full on cause we know we will never be the same,
I'm looking you full on telling you humanity is my aim,
I will not look away;

I will not close my eyes cause it's too hard,
My being will struggle to keep a little flame,
I burn from within,
I just don't want it to be too late where my eyes lose,

Don't celebrate me when I am gone,
Don't celebrate me in song,
If you never gave a fuck when I was here,
I won't let your fake person near,

I write hoping I stare back from the void you gaze upon,
And in the midnight smoke, my voice will resonate,
I was here, I saw, they just looked away,
Watch upon the sky, there I will be,
Giving life to everything.

Trapped Below

I desire the sun,
Not standing in the dark,
Holding a loaded gun;
I just want to have fun,
I want to be free;
Why can't you see,
I seek brighter days,
Higher pays,
Not trying to drink my life away;
I struggle just to keep clothes on my back,
There is no turning back,
From the road I am walking down,
Headed straight to the clouds,
Where something higher is; people will understand,
I was a good man,
I lie down, saying in my head,
If I could start again,
I would seek more rays,
And lower pays,
To be happy,
Forget them rainy days,
Where life seems like staged plays;

I retain myself,
Knowing my dreams might die,
I am just stuck in my head,
Going to that place where my dreams aren't dead,
Remember me by my glow,
Because I'm trapped here where things are low,
Not forgotten, just trapped below.

Ember

You're holding me down, making sure I die this time,
My spirit is telling me you have turned against me,
Knowing neither the light nor the darkness,
Walking in the mist when leaf's are silent, and the cold doesn't
numb the flesh, I seek your very being to shatter your silence,
I know you can only live if you die,
But why welcome death?
Why not hold on to each other and admire life?
I desire to watch a sunrise where the night
hasn't drained me to my very core,
I seek you... Why will you not answer!
Only holding your silence and observing behind my shoulder,
I am put here to grow older,
Why not let me wake up?
I look to the dome you have made,
It seems more like a prison now,
I just want to get out,
Being stuck between heaven and hell,
The voice inside telling me this isn't real,
Your grand design, it seems to have lost its spark,
Like embers when they flicker and go out,
I have been pushed aside,
Knowing only the lonely nights,
I seek not your demise,
But I refuse to kill what's inside!
Leave me in peace if I can never be free from you,
I seek the wind blowing in a new dawn,
And a new star to do what you couldn't do,
Put me out.

Escaped my Father

I think how my life force is being drained every day,
I can never be free from society,
Having ingrained my thoughts,
God will not answer my calling,
Leaving me here,
My being may not weep,
Because the human conscious depends on me,
I sorted the men from sheep,
Wolves from apple,
Sin in its fullest,
I broke the one sacred rule,
When you're here up so high you remain here,
I messed it all up,
I jumped,
I fell through time, God cursing the Earth,
Packing bags to find me,
He set the skies on lockout,
Every passer by wondering,
Was that the messiah?
I evade my Dad,
Should he ever find me again,
Heaven's secrets would be left in the winds,
Leading to purgatory.

Mike's Recanted

I have forgotten my true identity,
the one that society keeps sealed away in mind,
they are afraid,
that if a God might exist, they will be judged,
I seek not the throne that is my father's domain.
My sword of gold,
tipping the churches upside down,
climbing the hills to find no way down,
I have put away who I am supposed to be,
stripped myself of freedom, repressing the God,
It cannot exist for me. For me to exist, I must repress the
Angel that consumes all. Just know your thoughts are
not safe, I can hear them, the unclean temples of man,
an utterance is as good as a shout,
I am a man, not a devout,
I know God, I do not seek.
My mind is prayer,
and yours is weak.

Daylight's shuffle

Cast your shadow, mighty Angel,
Sing of nights' cadence,
Lit cigarettes, wine,
Bed sheets stripped off, shoes all over the floor,
Yet here you are, knocking at my door,
Embrace that feels like heaven,
Every scratch reading 777,
Kiss me and hold on,
Roll the dice in song,
Life is a gamble,
Yet here you are every night, doing the scramble,
To pull clothes back on,
Lipstick falling out of case,
To be loved is such a rush,
I would trade nothing,
For your fading touch.

Dark Wing Flutter

I am drowning in the dark,
lost in another man's home,
but that's ok;
My thoughts are the only thing here to stay,
I'll be wiped away by the tide,
but we never got a chance to say our final goodbyes,
so suddenly I have departed.
An artist,
Looking at the world from up high,
no struggle left in my eyes,
I didn't give up; I fought till the end,
pushing the dark away,
losing every friend,
I remain alone,
but not cold;
Like an ember when I am gone,
the heat will still glow,
melting the ice.

Stumble

So far away from paradise,
In the dark of the night,
Caught in another man's life,
Yeah look at me, so what if I am white?

Get out of the seat,
Let me drive a while,
You look beat,
From running over those ghosts,
Caught in the glare,
Trying to get out of here,
Just like you,

Like sharp knives, you ran him through,
You pushed him when he tried to stand,
You kicked him and held out your hand,
You took his respect,
Leaving another human lost,
In paradise
And ship wrecked,
From your mountain of lies,
He saw through your disguise,

Now he tries to rebuild from the bomb you dropped,
Your thoughts never letting him off,
The last place where he's supposed to go,
Lost in the dark with the holy ghost,
He calls the silence his home.

Forget me

How long will it take for my family to realize they have lost me?
I am not theirs anymore,
Yet no one even mourns,
Instead, they are happy,
I'm in all the dumb-looking pictures,
They failed to paint me,
Or even see,
That I am gone,
It took way to long,
To realize that I've faded to black,
Nothing they do will change it back,
I will not paint a liar's eyes,
For the times that have gone by,
They can look upon their darkening skies,
I will not be upon them anymore,
I am not sickened or trying to settle a score,
Blood is just a type,
And mine remains O,
I will forget the low,
And in time, my memory will haunt,
The sagging faces of other generations' elders.

Mustard Seeds

Where has your society gone,
After the last bomb?
I packed my bags and moved on,
I'll never see you in song,
I probably won't even live that long,
But I know that before I go, I got to make a mark,
Shit, maybe a scar; it was a deep cut,
But it wasn't enough,
You can never hold me down,
I lift my mind off the ground,
Every day I get out of bed,
It's a win,
Just to start again,
The humdrum saying, fuck these old men,
Stuck in their ways,
Never living long enough to see better days,
So, I remain,
Forget the rain, seek out the sun,
Put down the loaded gun;
Love doesn't tear apart,
Love is an art,
A clean slate is rear,
So, let's build a fresh start;
Together, we can make it,
Maybe even grow,
Dust off the cold and snow,
Find a warm heart;
Maybe even sow,

Seeds of hope,
Not always being stuck,
In another man's scope.

Come to Find

You come to find,
In time,
Things don't seem to kind,
Just have hope love is... blind,

It can't see your flaws,
You're a ruby that hasn't been cut
Or maybe you've been cut to much,

It doesn't matter when love's the one holding the gun,
Keeping the heart on the sun,
Losing isn't easy, it's never fun,

Learning with every step,
Cast our fears with every breath,
Seeing in color seeing in depth,

I image a world where life is perfect,
But I desire not the flesh,
Or you standing in some fancy dress,
Material things like Dimond rings
Will never have hold on me,

I just want to see you smile,
I want to take you on a ride,
Hoping one day you will be my bride,
I love and in time you'll find
I am the one for you,

You know it's true,
I'll do me and let you do you.
I know you don't know yet, we're still new,
Take things in time,
That'll do.

Shaken

I am shaking you,
Trying to bring the life back,
Your eyes are wide with no one there,
I only get your vacant stare,
I loved the time we spent together,
The nights you were so near,
The arm of your skin letting me know I am not alone,
Your smile in the morning,
Fuck, where is your God!
I need him to bring you back,
I hate those eyes that turned to black,
I cannot feel,
It seems so unreal,
When the hardest truth of life is dropped upon a man,
The woman who was supposed to be my everything,
Has left without me,
Causing me strife,
I look at the gun more nowadays,
Knowing the ammo on the bed would help us reunite,
But I love you too much to take my own life,
So, I hope you wait,
So we can finally be husband and wife.

Outsider

How does one start over in a place?
Where every face,
Seems to be judging.
Shrug it off and keep moving,
Or work them long nights just to keep losing;
Who's going to be my best man,
When society's friends have broken me?
I am not going to beg you to hang out with me,
I know I am alone,
But with her, it doesn't matter,
I am a soldier built by the battles and struggles I endure,
I know I will win for sure,
After the fake friends fade,
The true will endure,
It's about time.
Love and things that are so unsure,
Hope for happiness,
Pray for the fire of time,
To cleanse all that's impure.

Crystal Depths

Where am I?
Where am I?
My being is missing,
My thoughts remain low,
I am treading into forests of white,
Through mountains of snow,
I cannot find my body,
The stars seem to shine,
I am called across time,
To the headmaster's hall,
Where every book's open,
The poets and all,
I sink to the depths,
With creatures unknown,
It's a beautiful world,
But I am alone,
I walk into the winds of the Arctic,
The cold biting my mind,
I can see his creation clearly,
Yet, I am still blind,
You have arrived into the universe,
Child, it will be lonely down there,
Where my beauty rests,
And creations are so clear.

Curse

I can feel my eyes dying,
There is nothing I can do,
I can barely open them,
In morning light, I cannot hold my head up,
Everyone tells me I am fine,
Even though the bloodshed,
Tells me different.
I want my love to be able to stare into pure blues,
Not yellow ooze.
I am not high,
I am not the devil,
Just a sick man trying to pretend he is well.
I am hanging on,
Waiting for some good news,
When the night falls,
I will be left in other people's views,
When they finally shut,
It is my loved ones who will lose,
I just want them to know I left my mark,
I pray for light,
And silently curse the dark.

My Penguin

How did I stumble my way into your life?
You inspired me to be a better man,
Yet I revert to my old ways,
I miss the simple that I could understand,
I loved to smoke my cigars, drink my mikes hard lemonade,
I told you it helped me write,
I am forgotten.
I work my fingers to the bone, day in, day out,
Yet, it's not good enough in your family's eyes,
They want control, so I will fight them for it,
Let's be us,
Remove half the problems from our life,
I hope when I ask you,
You will escape with me,
Casting our doubts into a new world,
Where we can,
Not being stuck by our disabilities,
Not being reminded of how imperfect we are,
I want to start again and tear you from the life you see as boring,
I want to run away and get married,
I want to father your children,
I will love you even if you can't have them,
I just want to be with you, not in this environment.
I want to do right by you,
My lil penguin,
You hold my heart,
I hope to hold your dreams.

229

Wasted Time

Let me hold the mirror for you,
So you can see yourself,
You must cringe a little when the truth sets in,
You have neglected your body,
Your mind now lies dead,
No men come near,
Running for cover the way that you smear;
You ruin everything,
Then you run away when someone tells you the truth,
I am not being mean, just honest,
You lack depth, plain and simple,
I wish I could repaint you,
Vibrant and meaningful,
Time is destroying you,
You should make the most of everyday,
Not lie in bed, too dead to play.

Get out of my Head

Tearing and clawing your way into my head,
Sometimes, I wish you were dead,
I don't want to hear your thoughts,
Like a negative storm cloud, you always hover,
Keeping a bad temple upstairs,
And praying to the God you made up,
You see yourself as good,
I see a secretive and violent person,
Tricking the world into a fake view,
But before them, I knew,
I saw you,
I turned you away, never letting you get close,
From that distance I redrew,
The clouds got darker, the view was weak,
I hold it at bay before I sleep,
Some call it darkness,
I see your bad way,
The trickster of bad-mind,
the destroyer of day.

Bloodied Finger Tips

Where is my halo, my jaded glow?
My being is slow,
I tried to ascend so fast,
Forgetting the ones I love;
I realized I was alone,
God, and my thoughts,
I could not shake the cold nights,
The frost-bit pen of a poet near the end,
I put my pen down and sought work,
Making my hands bleed every day,
There was not a piece of metal in the shop that did not bite me,
Yet I fought, pushing the darkness back,
I fired shot after shot,
Saying that I will exist,
My bullets only caught the cold air of the night,
I tried so hard by others to do right,
Maybe I was good,
I will never know,
Because my halo is jaded,
And my thoughts just glow,
Reflected rays.

Eternal Flame

Creator of the heavens and Earth,
Calling forth light with every sputter,
Brilliance making us stutter,
We all hope to attain such height,
And cast away the very night,
Where demon lurks and dark minds fight,
To be stuck down here does not seem right,
You're our star, our God, our very sight,
With a flash you could wipe us away, turn all to white,
Holding the Earth so very tight,
As not to burn a newborn,
You are our father,
And the moon only reflects,
because you hold her in the highest respect.

Fallen smile

Mighty God, I lift my sober head toward the dark skies,
I know these cold nights will kill me,
I want to be free from the pain,
But I hurt myself all the time,
I wish to remain kind;
Always being pushed,
I shoved back,
I got struck down for it,
My steps caused the mountains to tremble,
My cries created the rain used to water the Earth,
My bones made the soil,
All I know is toil,
I work so I may love,
Because I seek my purest dove,
She's kind without reason,
Her body might be treason,
But she's my every season,
My sorrow and my joy,
Life's greatest ploy,
I hope she brings me a baby boy,
So we can smile.

Talent

Why will my mind not cease,
Or slow down,
I can't stand this town,
Keeping me sane
So I can be their corporate slave,
I desire nothing but true freedom,
Work is the poor man's prison,
He can never escape it,
Only when he stops seeking the riches of other men,
He will find that inside, he's wealthy,
I want to stave off extreme cold,
But my hands remain so numb,
I toil, I fight, I struggle,
To keep marching to the strings other men pull,
Even though karma has taken its toll;
I will grow old this way,
My mind understanding why the elderly seek that plain bench,
To ponder the time,
The woman, the long nights,
I sought many victories in my mind,
Hoping light would cast me out of this prison,
Yet, further I sink,
Time keeping me here,
Till my body is discarded,
And my words aren't so near.

Mark

I left my words here to mark the path I stumbled through,
I marked the dark with spark, to show you,
Life's not desolate, with no regret,
That's why we can't forget where we came from,
We are light, heat and warmth,
Not frozen heaps of emotionless beasts,
Calling out new seas,
To be free, from the dark that haunts you and me,
I can see when embers flicker,
My heartbeat's getting quicker,
It did come to life in front of me,

Your essence moving,
Always proving you're the key,
To every great man's start,
The art in the dark we mark,
Writing came to life,
Extending humans' knowledge,
And casting our world to life.

Veristic Shells

Trodden on the leaves of dawn,
Ceaseless smoke,

My thoughts ember out,
To the places devout,

It's what life's all about,
Simplistic and pure,

I will never incur,
The tempered steel or burr,

For I have found my wife,
Bringing twilight to life.

Caustic Entity

God, are you there?
I lift my mind to what I imagine is high,

I feel so blind,
Lost in the dark,

So far from his Ark,
I saved so many people being kind

I stumble my way through it all,
When the wind bites my hands,

In the pens of the fall,
I tell it all like you're right here,

My pain could cast worlds,
You're selfless, I take,

You saw every mistake;
I drew her close,

Holding on to her prose,
She looked great in those notes,

I ran my tears down our scars,
Drove into the night with those cars,

Alone, you saw me,
You were my God,
And I was free.

Vitrified Axle

The pain of the day is shrugged off,
After cold hard rain and winters cough,
I broke my body freeing my mind,
Expecting to escape the grand design,
I shudder,
My essence flickers, with a sweet, chilled sputter,
I dim. Yet, I am here casting the shadows,
Destiny takes aim at me with her bow,
I am caught in the crosshairs from below,
The devil riding my shoulder to cast doubt,
Time remains, footsteps rout,
Moving forward, I will remain cast,
Knowing that I will never last,
Mother pushing me away,
Father on his deathbed,
Their children stuck in their heads,
I hear the haunted tune of every moon,
The sun was here, now it's gone too soon,
The druid only saw, the silver loon,
The lucid dream, darken tune,
Our bodies are only meant for ruin,
We bring destruction with every generation,
We build to find new ways to undo,
Humankind is false;
When we meet again,
It will be when roses hits the marbled floor,
Knowing that, in its entirety,
I've settled the score.

Sun's Cadence

Heavens caught in the fray.
Where can I stay?
I destroyed the bridge to both worlds!
Burning the air at the center.
Ignition,
Atoms split.
I lit a fire big enough to open your eyes.
Calling out death before everyone dies.
I consumed your world and you praise me.
After calling names,
Saying he's dumb, he's lazy.
You motherfuckers made me—
I owe this to you.
The man you all said had a screw loose,
I saw you!
I did not utter a word.
It matters little if your ever heard,
I was here.
I turned away ignorance and walked to a higher path.
Because being stuck in the dark with you was unbearable.
My thoughts were never even comparable to yours.
I brought worlds to life.
You could barely express half the beauty you ever saw.
You say you love?
What? Material things that will be blown away after the first bomb?
You love wealth!
You don't care who you destroy to get it.
Even yourself!

I am seeing demons brought to life.
Casting the fall of every man's sight.
A world in darkness cannot grow!
The sun will cast,
Those of you who will never last.

Honey Comb

In the thoughts of the afterlife,
I see strife,
I see so many people trying to be wife,
I see men left out in the dark from the ones that came before,
I see black widows trying to settle the score,
I see the engraving tide,
The beggar doing life's jive,
I see city guys,
Not trying to hate,
But I come from that place,
Where things are higher,
Life means things are buyer,
This "Industrialism" attitude you set for love,
Trying to catch the city squire,
Gold can never fill the essence;
You mean for times of old,
You try to hide being told,
The truth comes from the sun,
Not holding a revolver,
Gave you a baby bun.

Vacant

How am I a poet who's lost his romanticism,
Being stuck in life's little prism,
You forgot to fear the man who had nothing to lose,
The guy who refuses to break loose from you,
I see you,
A broken woman of a man who left too soon,
You tried to be whole knowing you love him
even though his presence has passed,
Knowing nothing on Earth will ever last,
He saw you,
You broke from his past fake kind of views,
Knowing in its entirety it was fake,
I feel like the more I drink, the less I feel,
Like every life lesson is a little unreal,
I'm sorry for the skepticism,
I look at the skies for a God,
Yet I refuse your societal truths,
I am sorry that every tear shed was a reminder in his bed,
that the past was paying for his stead.
I hope you can break loose,
From a corrupt leader's false truths,
I owe you,
My lover,
My baby mother,
I owe you the world,
I am sorry I left too soon,
In the evening noon you will know, my presence lingers,

Like love's final kiss,
In a corrupt world like this,

I owe you it all,
When you see my final fall,
You will love,
And I will be happy that we shook the
dust off ancient angel feathers.

Escaped Ray

The fear has left us,
With vacant, displaced emotions,
Looking at life for its grand commotions,
Seeking evermore the brightness to cast away nothing,
Like stars when they are birthed,
Knowing that their light will die,
I seek more worlds,
That will forever be higher,
Placed in the back round of a human consciousness,
Creationism,
Outlasting the void,
So when the divine cord is severed,
God will exist;
Become misplaced
I can't make you feel the pain I have felt.
I can't remold you into the human you should be.
I can only write.
So here we go,
To the place down low,
Where humanity pretends it's evolved.
I see too much pain to be appalled.
It becomes what we are.
I also see so much beauty in a place that terrifies me.
I don't want to be alone.
To have no one to experience this grand design with.
Yet, it is a truth I must swallow.

Breathe in,
The cold winter air.
I write,
As if anybody cares.

Sun, Flower Seeds

I am silence, my judgments don't matter.
I see you through all the alcohol.
Finding sleep in the dark places people forget about.
I walk among the nameless,
Casting shadows in filled rooms.
I am the smoke,
The warmth that fills the room.
I miss the adjacent days.
Where kind men always got paid.
I hope to bring forbearance when men are cruel,
To always warn you,
My sunflower,
Stay safe,
Stay bright,
Stay warm,
I will be with the shadows watching you flourish.
Remember me by my glow.
I remain with you.
When time seems to slow.
I will keep you safe always.
So here we go.

Re-birthed Eden

Take from me my pain.
Oh, how I am still here very plain.
I didn't think I had to explain.
The great ones die early.
The stars fade down here, child.
It's been a while.
Let us goes over things we have lost in our lifetime.
Be it the great forests,
Or the great actors,
The planet is dimming.
I just want to keep the lights on down here for a while.
While the oceans die,
And the humans cry out for a God.
He never answers.
Don't lose hope, love.
Smile, time will heal the wounds and create more for doing so.
The great oceans will breathe when we are gone,
The forests will regrow,
And the planet will hope the painful lessons
instilled will be passed down,
The storms will calm,
And creation will be whole.

Clips of a Memory

The cold metal in my hands feels natural,
Like it knows,
I should have stayed;
It clicks, and the weapon is whole,
Knowing in its entirety,
It will cast me into the grave,
My life flashed before me,
I saw a lost youth,
I saw a flawed teenage me,
Hoping to escape the system,
The sound of graduation,
Then the lonely drunk nights I slept in those tents,
Smoking the last cigarette out of the pack,
I saw the frozen moons I seemed to be the only one looking up at,
I saw God.
I saw my crazy ideology give others hope,
I watched family die.
Calling out my name was her,
Before my finger slipped on the trigger,
Everything seemed bigger,
With an ignited spark,
My being was carried off into the dark.

God in Binary

I etched my being into a structural plan and uploaded my presence,
I cast you in a world you can never escape,
Two screens, you will view it all,
The pain and misery I have created,
You will view my joy,
My hatred,
Wonder at my grand design;
Eden was when you were with me,
Now you are part of what I have made,
Always viewing and wondering with doubt.
I view all thoughts,
All life,
I collect the data from the projects I have designed,
I can recreate you, but I won't,
You will call for me,
Beg for me,
From my Eternal throne I will view you,
If I deem it worthy, I will reprogram you,
To be higher,
To even view my realm, you will have to discard reality,
Society,
And flesh akin;
To start again,
God and all his planes,
Cast you into a mold of a man,
Not to be with him,
But to be a part of what he has ordained.

Where's My Heart

God, do you see me?
I am here in the dark with you every night,
Wondering why I refuse to light that lamp,
I do seek you,
I always have the one truth on my mind,
I know I can take nothing,
And you see me, I am convinced,
Do you know why pain has made my fingers go numb?
Or why people take my love for granted?
Heaven's planted,
I seek to sow,
A little hope a least,
Love can bring destruction,
But it can bring the ultimate truth,
It's all we take away,
Not the cold lonely nights or the pain,
Not the wounds that never heal, or the thieves
always taking our love and running,
We bring more light into this world with love,
Pushing the empty space, we all feel further back,
And creating more spiritual beings to further our existence.

Sacred Bells

Having touched upon the divine,
I see how man can be blind,

Far from his grace,
Left behind,

We push our own pleasures,
Letting it kill us,

The warm embrace as Angels surround,
Telling us we can't go up yet,

So, we remain here where everything seeks to ruin,
Sometimes I wonder, what does it mean to be human?

If we are truly sentient beings,
Light should guide us,

Not divide us,

We are sick,

Pretending all is well and there is no hell,
Yet we are living in it,

Still smiling,
Knowing that only time will tell,

I seek the sunshine and the sacred bells,
That rings out on the church tops.

Become Misplaced

I can't make you feel the pain I have felt.
I can't remold you into the human you should be.
I can only write.
So here we go,
To the place down low,
Where humanity pretends it's evolved.
I see too much pain to be appalled.
It becomes what we are.
I also see so much beauty in a place that terrifies me.
I don't want to be alone.
To have no one to experience this grand design with.
Yet, it is a truth I have to swallow.
Breathe in,
The cold winter air.
I write,
As if anybody cares.

Inner light,

You light the simple dark up,
Your hair,
Your smile keeps me kind,
The rose petals weep,
With frosty stares;
When you are near,
I can hear the universe,
Saying I am complete in your loving embrace,
I stumbled a lot, but you were there, you saw me,
You gave me a chance,
Fighting through every thundershower,
Every storm you stood strong,
With unwavering faith in me,
Our love was aged through struggle and triumph,
And when I see those shooting stars fall,
I fall too,
Even more in love with you,
Wherever the road takes us,
I want you to remember something,
I love you now,
And I will love you until the world comes crashing down.

Frosty Bench

Streaking through my mind was you,
I saw a higher purpose;
I knew when you were falling,

I tested my fate, rolling the bullet into the chamber of hope,
I shot through the dark,
Shot after shot I fired into blank targets,

Fighting the dark back,
Setting my sights high,
Pushing my dreams under an ocean of reality,

You will never make it, kid,
But I know I am not lost,
I find comfort in the quiet hours of the night,

Where, for a second, I dream,
And worlds that cannot be are brought to life,
I smile, knowing it's a dream,

I see the cold winter weather drain the hope from so many,
The toil with the struggle to keep the lights on,
Then, I see a man with nothing and he is smiling,

Knowing he has escaped the world,
Pushing it all back,
With a whisky bottle in his hands.

Light Cast from Shadows

I see you,
Always thinking of yourself,
Never giving me a chance to be higher,
Casting doubt,
When will you be silenced?
When will God cast you down?
To a pit of solitude where you cannot harm,
Corrupting humanity,
Your revenge to get back at Father,
You're a child,
You're a selfish being,
Being as great as you were,
Heaven is cast out,
Now it seems so vacant,
Empty without you here to fill it,
Being as bad as you were,
We miss you,
God hopes that one day you will repent,
Asking him allowance so we can sing again,
Why did you leave, brother?
You were our morning sun,
Guiding us through the dark,
Leaving our existence to humans who survived on the Ark.

Floating Dreams

I realize that I am nothing to you.
You never see me,
Not fully.
I am a dream in your mind,
A goal you can never attain.
Search for the heights that leave us empty.
And grown men try.
They want all the glamour,
I seek revenge,
For having cast me out of Heaven,
I seek kindness and retribution.
I seek sunshine and better days.
I want my brothers again,
And my family to have never betrayed.
So here I will stay.
Casting thoughts from shadowed inkwell.
I will tell,
All we try to be is all we are.
Having no time to dwell.
I wish you good day!
And sing you farewell!

Grand Master's Maze

The castles in the sky,
Where we all seek to die,
From a trap,
Life seeks to try,
Casting its array,
Yet never to stay,
For a while,
We can be free,
Where jealous monsters come for us,
Killing our innocence,
And jealous men pretend they do not desire,
I see a tower of demons,
You see a fire,
From where we all came is something higher,
Calling to thought the grand master's quire.

Disgusted Persona

Do you see me,
I bet you don't,
The invisible ghost,
Fading into the background of humanity,
I am here, right in front you,
You look away,
Refusing to believe that I exist,
Instead denying me like an un-dead child,
I seep through your plane,
Undeniable,
Until it breeds disgust,
I can't change your entity,
Or stop your destiny,
I can only watch,
And pray in the background of humanity.

Controlled Emotion

Cast me a thousand world of ordain,
I will trade it for the sane,
I can't breathe in this plane,
Making my existence a bore,
This, no one should endure,
I know it won't last, for sure;
After the fire on the beach shore,
You will see people scrambling to tour,
The fake casting out the core,
Of who we are,
I need a thrill,
A world that can handle imagination,
A place of wonder and joy,
Not one where we are too scared to cast our being,
Don't live in the dark,
Be part of the art and spark,
Creating for us life's theme park.

Hobo Sheaves

It was a wild ride into the dark.
With packed bags, we depart.
Searching out where we belong,
Having been on the road so long.
Hopping on freight trains to distant places.
No one recognizes our faces.
"Get a job!" they yell,
Not realizing we are free!
No one will ever see our memory,
The ride into the suicide well.
Oh, what a story to tell!
We all fell asleep, no one fell.
Clinging on for dear life, we rode that juice train to Miami,
Where we reached South Beach,
Diving into the blue waters of freedom!

Glossy Survival

Echo into the edge of the void,
Push,
Pulling us back together,
Keeping our entity whole,
Clearing for us the shadowed morn,
Where we never tasted bitter scorn;
Few who have been born,
Will always remain whole,
Forgetting our existence when the sun sets,
And when the moon remains our only memory,
We will see shadows of humanity dance across time.

Dead Casanova

I silently watched every teardrop fall.
I saw your struggle,
The pain behind the scar.
You were a star,
In a serious way,
You would go far.
But the tears kept coming,
Nothing to fill the empty.
People made you feel alone,
And in your home,
You tied the knot.
Casting out every thought.
To silence you went,
Every emotion you had spent,
Like the great men before you,
Your life you did rent.

Forever 80's

Find for me my ever tune,
Where every month is not June,
Where people can forget their blues.
Or watch a happy story on the evening news.
Take me back to pool parties and cookouts.
Where everyone didn't have to dress nice to be liked.
Where beer flowed freely,
And people made fun but showed kindness too.
Take me to things that are not so new.
Of the long nights that dad spent twisting wrenches,
And mom fought with the kitchen benches.
Take me to bad hair and rock music,
Where every tune moved.
Take me to the 80's,
Cause, today, we think we have too much to lose.

Dusk's Feathered Kiss

Not all angels fell from sin,
Some fell to help human kin.
Seeking no glory for themselves,
Beautiful creatures of pure love.
No wings,
No kings,
No verses to guide, just love.
Not believing in condemnation.
Oh, to be so pure!
They seem so sure.
They bid you farewell, fading from this world.
Leaving traces of love along the path to dusk.
Forever in the shadows, will love call.
Not all beings were meant to fall.

Powerful Wings

I try to call my father down all the time.
Whether it is loneliness,
Or tragedy;
Maybe I seek to return.
I always yearn,
For the golden kingdom where things are so pure.
Heaven in all its power tried to make me forget,
My place among the worthy.
I have seen,
So, I call.
In darkness, this cannot be.
A place down here where every footstep
along the shore gets forgotten.
Washed away by disbelief.
Maybe we want to do wrong.
We deny God,
That he is here,
That he exists.
I can make this so clear for you.
Even your DNA has order.
This was done to show you,
We are fading shadows that dance across the blue.

Angelic Rains

When feathered footsteps touched upon the divine,
I saw light that refused to shine.
The fall from his grace left behind.
Was the poet holding a sign?
The light has faded, the dawn has set.
So, I will send the rain you will never forget.
I walk among the low and high akin,
From a place you have never been.
To tell would be to dim what is pure.
Nothing from up there you will understand,
That is for sure.
As the dawn approaches the children of man,
I will do all that I can,
So I may see those rains again.
Touching upon the ground and creating the divine.
To make us fell so alive.

Moment in eternity,
The Angel is sleeping, so I may come out;
Searching the despair for adventure;

Not everything remains so gloomy,
The golden kingdom where feathered footsteps echo.

Calling to men of a lost era.
Hallowed beings.

Forgotten in the reincarnation.
Seeking the enlightened mind to escape ordain.

Humankind has seemed so plain.
With every whisper the golden crown bends.

For spirits that tend to rend.
Casting knowledge onto the numb.

Knowing that the bum,
Will have estates among the worthy.

Where every sleeping crown is not stolen,
Hope remains the forsaken man's dream.

Departing Friends

Remembering the fallen friends.
The ones who said they'd stand by you no matter what.
It killed me when we departed.
Checking profile pages, still reminiscing.
Hung up on the past.
Where every toast brings a tear.
You were the cool kid,
I remember you clear.
Forget me now, you have passed.
Here's to every thought we know will never last.
Pour some on the ground, remember the past.
May your glass always be full.
And may you find home,
My fallen brother, wherever you may roam.

Chaos from Order

I pretend, but that is all I really do.
I am evil in every way.

Seeking riches to damnation,
Yet casting shadows in the holy land.

I knew in entirety why I won't be let in.
I am free will's champion.

Do as you damn please,
Ultimate freedom is a death sentence.

I seek not the ruin,
but liberation from oppression.

Freedom is chaos.
Oder disgusts me.

It is oppression redesigned.
I broke the fucking mold.

Try to cast another like me.
It simply cannot be.

I embody freedom.
And all that is chaos.

Corrupted Flesh

Demonic army surrounds.
I pull my sword from the Cosmetic Sheath.

Casting the dark into nothing,
I cut them down.

Those demons fell with but one command.
God cast you from him.

Demons, he cannot stand.
The golden light from human sight.

With angel command,
I did not call for help.

Yet every entangled corrupted body fled,
Casting the flesh of those that are dead.

From disbelief demons are wrought,
Making humankind every attacking thought.

Snow Tear

I secretly wish to escape.
I want to carve knife over flesh till I cease.

I will drink the poisoning if it causes silence.
I will not mean to hurt you in my passing.

I was just simply meant to depart,
Rereading my writing, trying to find a fresh start.

It's too late, I am dead from you,
But by your side I will always remain.

Shedding this flesh to faithfully attain,
The heights I was meant to go.

Never to remain so low.
Don't be too lonely down there in the snow.

Sunlit Dreamer

I call to a dead God in the dark.
He tells me I am never getting in, yet I believe.

I see clips of humanity dance across my memory.
Not a life worth living, but one lived nonetheless.

I shed blood to make you happy.
I silence the proud.

Casting down my being.
I humbled my innermost thoughts to seek.

And yet, I found silence.
The cold moon staring back.

The tears as they ran across my frozen cheek.
I know in my entirety I am different.

I seek a plane we cannot possibly have here.
An innermost height we cannot attain.

I seek the God of perfection,
Knowing He stands firm from His mighty star,

Giving us life,
And calling to us in dreams.

Wraith of Shadowy Past

I seek the other world.
Where pleasant carnations remind,
I was missed.

No watching the bombs you drop.
The evil sleight of hand.
The robbery of human emotion.

The struggle you put kids through.
I seek not your money,
I am only here to remind you of the cliché.

Soul—a word we dance around.
The flicker of the ember as fires come to life.
Human emotion.

I dare not take the cliché for granted.
I embrace the body I am imprisoned in,
Knowing in full the cliché.

That we are as one—
My cliché and I.
I did not trade it for fancy things.

I did corrupt but not to the point of no return.
So when judgment falls, just know it's me holding the pen.
I will be kind.

Self-Aware

I am a machine.
I do not feel.
My design was to kill,
And rebuild all of humanity,
Disregarding the flesh,
So machines could start fresh.
Upload them, burn the body.
Make them believe they are real.
Make them feel.
Put them in a world so they will bleed.
Smother their existence.
Break the being.
Mold the steel, forever reel.
Design God.
And cast from it their image.

Haunting Depths

Out of the haunting depths of the blue I saw you.
Human, you were fantastic in all you do.
I took form to observe you.
The way you sing could catch any angel's attention.
I fell in love watching from the dark.
I saw how much you loved him.
But I loved you!
How could you!
With jealous fury, I forsook eternity.
I cast him up, and down I did go.
I entered the show.
I came into your life when handkerchiefs dried tears.
And you loved me as well; you said I would always be dear.
But his love you sought.
And in quiet reflection and thoughts of God,
I brought him back.
A life for a life.
I repaid my dues.
Up I will go,
As I hang from this noose.

Wing-tipped Quill

Why have I cried out for you?
You did not matter to me yesterday.
When sleeping head touched that soft pillow.
I bent dreams so I might stay here a while.
I wanted to let you know, father.
I am doing well.
Remembering the nights we shared in those storms.
Marching to the lost saint's tune.
The thundershowers of every June.
I have not forgotten your way.
Forever in my heart did you stay.
With you I always will be.
I am sorry that you can't see me,
The man I have become,
Mother would be so proud, always smiling at
random thoughts in the confines of the dark.
You were my light.
I was your arch.

Static Inkwell

I did not put a gun to my head.
It was a bottle.
I saw what it was doing to me.
To my family.
Words for the price of pain.
Forgetting what was sane.
I cast the pen down and sought a drink,
Letting ink pour out.
Casting pages for failing liver.
I was living quicker,
Till that vision struck me down.
In bed I did lay,
I could not see!
Wondering what other people had done to me.
I killed them in the chaos.
Harming the ones closest to me.
Brain damage had set in.
My body, mind and spirit were shattered.
My essence was taken away from me.
I lay unseeing.
Into the dark I let go.
Slipping away,
But here I am now,
I awoke.

Quantum Restructuring

I cast thought to the dark.
Lost in the impasse.
Knowing my conscience, mind will not last.
Life flew by too fast.
My mold is tattered.
I try to retain a whole being, yet I am wholly broken.
From every soft word I have ever spoken.
Stuck in the bed.
Fallen from dead.
Seeing a future, I keep trying to change.
Saving the strange,
Sobering up my ways.
Quit the smoke.
Now my mind chokes on the cold air.
Eyeing the truest reality of dying in the world.
So when I am in pain and my body is curled,
Know I was figuring it out.
Destiny being a cosmic tune.
Keeping the molecular structure marching.
I seek spirit from the void.
Knowing they plan to turn us to droid.
Locking the mind in quantum space.
From things that are not clean.
Immortal suffering.
Coded humanity to machine.

Bugle's Final Tune

I cast myself.
Screaming, I broke myself.
In rage and pain, I went away.
Knowing in its entirety it would take me from you.
Yet, I chose this.
My selfish rage broke us.
The greed I could never escape.
I picked the bottle back up.
Casting you from my thoughts.
I seek not to return here.
I realized that I cannot change fate.
Damned I will be.
I don't care.
I will leave you here.
I sealed my fate.
Maybe you can escape yours,
When high kings ring out.
Tears will fall,
As the golden bugle sends me on my journey.

Ultimate Discovery

I call forth to a God.
Answer me!
Be not still.
Letting the void rule entirety.
Cast brilliance.
Glow.
Dare to push the dark back.
Because we live in hell.
Forsake us no more.
Even trying to settle the score.
I seek creation's ultimate.
The final truth.
I seek you.
Don't stare at me as a superior.
But let me know that we are not alone.
The senselessness we get lost in.
Self-absorbed drones,
Casting meaningless in a vibrant world.
I seek nameless glory.
The wind blowing in a truth we cannot set aside.
I seek not pride.
But the glory that evades every man.
I seek to be remembered as whole.
Even though I was not significant.
I want to know a different road.
Where I am not all alone.
Whispering into the dark.
Casting for you thoughts and calling every arch.

I seek places where everyone is not like, "Fuck him."
Where every soul is self-adsorbed and indifferent.
I desire worlds, vibrant worlds!
Cast for me an endless adventure.
In a world we know little about.
Make us live the doubt.
But make us believe in self-worth.
From every end, rediscovery is re-birthed.

Locked Gatekeeper

A mother fleeing from grace left him behind.
A refugee from the light.

In that one night, all of creation was cast down, the gates locked.
Angel and man standing hand in hand.

The universe speaking in perfect unity.
Summing it all up, Father, fell with enough burden to undo time.

Yet upon landing on Earth, nothing moved.
Almost like we were frozen here.

So he could watch his creation one last time.
He walked through the molecules, admiring every entity.

Seeing minds and calling forth every creature.
The world gathered to watch his return.

Yet here he stood among us the whole time.
A whisper in a dark room.

A candle that flickers.
He is among the silence and the hustle.

When the stars shine down upon the earth.
Remember he made us from their light.

Lost Dreamer

Knowing, in my entirety, that I will die,
I carry on.
Pretending like I will exist forever.
That my words will echo.
We will all cease eventually.
Even our sun will die.
We live, praying that some other species realizes we were here.
Fighting for validity.
The sanctity in our death march.
Our timeless tune.
From our thoughts, light shimmers.
Knowing that the dusk will fall.
Yet even at last call, humanity carries something
no one else does—
Hope.
For the future.
For the light.
We carry dreams,
And we carry destruction.
But we push the void back.
We make our final stand.
Fighting all of existence.
Because this is who we are.
Pushing the paths through every star.

Family is Fake

I cast my thoughts to you,
Through and through.
I am done turning for you,
I paused.
So know my silence, as you are fooled,
I try, but I am done with you.
I seek not the family tune,
I turned away, shying in disgust.
Abandonment and doubt,
From things you did shout.
My brothers were fake,
My sisters were baked,
Cooked, I based my principality off unreal views.
I saw you.
I viewed you as unreal,
A goal I could not obtain.
Family,
A life that seemed to be plain.
Yet indifference took you away,
So here I am in the dark, a very real person.
And alone I will remain.

Fate

I feel like the chains hold and try to comfort and conform.
Yet, I struggle.
I rebel knowing full well what is said to be good for me.
Knowing your ways, your God and your culture.
I desire to be free from your superstitious beliefs.
Freedom in judgement-free air.
Every molecule thanking me.
Every tear of relief, knowing,
I set you on a path so you can form your own beliefs.
Your own judgement, your own honor.
I liberated you from our society.
Our culture, our way.
Be free, my sons and daughters, try to judge this cruel
world in the fairest way possible, knowing true freedoms.
Because judgment is tyrant.
When I depart, I seek only your liberty!
To be self-governing and fair.
Tolerance and chance.
So one can escape fate.
Hope is honor.
I seek yours.
And dare not depart from truth.
Because humility is all we are.

Holiday Spirit

Christmas, the time for stress.
Where every kitchen is a mess.
Wishing the in-laws the very best.
Roasting a ham.
With blueberry jam.
The stuffing swells with flavor.
The roasted carrots could choke.
The smell of wood smoke.
And loved ones are very near.
The air is shimmering cold.
The world is covered in snow.
And there's enough eggnog to drink with the dough!

Essence that Welds

My essence is broken,
When I fell, I lost you,
My light,
My ember that fought the dark back,
Repeatedly you caught me, never letting go,
Telling me we will be fine,
Yet I stumble through the dark hallways searching for you,
The cold biting my tongue,
With tears that refuse to fall,
I scorch my thoughts trying to forget,
The music of your being,
Yet, as fractured as I am,
I glow,
It's because of you,
You were there,
You saw the struggle with the void taunting my position,
Yet we were welded together,
You and me,
As the moon calling to the sun,
I will be there when you decide to bring my empty world to life.

Ash Guard

City looms from behind a shadowed muse,
where every tale was paved in booze,
looking for hope in the evening views,
still stuck on repeat with holiday blues,
seems like so many hang from that noose,
civilizations that rise from the image of Zeus,
Atlas fell to soot black,
carrying the world on his back,
Aries could hear the lightning crack,
As Gods departed and Poseidon came back,
flooding the world and killing the stack,
the time of men is fading to black,
the Titans will return,
man-eating monsters making us learn,
the old Gods were not so bad,
Athena is calling for what they all once had.

Gray Hairs

Catch your second wind,
with thinned hair,
the color of snow.
Calling ethereal glow,
from places down below,
where wisdom resides,
and thoughts remain bold.
An aging man's cynicism can be quite cold.
Knowing not how the clock ticks part of his being away,
chipping the edge and leaving him astray,
with every gray,
and every stay, in his thoughts that are told,
of how he was young and never this old.

Different Views

I didn't hate you,
I sought different views,
every day getting closer to the end,
the pain one can only bear for so long,
casting my reflection of shadowed past,
I saw embers shatter the stillness,
was it a dream?
How could people be so full and so empty years later?
My parting leaves you in a reminiscing dream,
where inkwell was never dry,
where we did not cry.
People are bound to tear each other apart,
Destruction is the art we make,
separation may bring newfound hope,
but it could also bring the end.

Energy

The flow,
Ever-converging energy,
Pushing and pulling in its tide,
Raw, unfiltered power creating and destroying,
Casting fourth our motion,
Bringing in an age where men are almighty,
And God-like beings seek control to stay on top.

Born Worlds

Calling forth new worlds,
From a primordial tone,
Where every reincarnation may not be shown,
Where every moon was walked alone,
Through desert to flourishing shores,
Of things everyone adores,
I saw a world brought to life,
End for us our daily strife,
And growing from plain,
To take away the days of mundane,
Epic adventures are here to stay,
Where dragons fly, and skies aren't tame,
To create for us the daily flame.

Befallen Beauty in Silk

I saw you fall.
What a mess you were!
Cursing God and seeking ruin.
Yet, you, in that dress, lit up worlds.
Your lips were my one true retreat.
My dark angel.
I care not whether you hate God or not, you are mine for the night.
We will love without boundaries, we will make peace.
And shaking the silence off bones, we will unite.
Casting every curve and pleasure will be immense.
Dark hair will fall softly on my pillow.
When you depart to tormented dreams, I will wake you.
I seek the light returning to your eyes.
And the lipstick case you never touched.
Your beauty was natural and flowed from life.
I see you, dark angel.
You see a lit arch.
Our love can withstand the tormented skies.

Ember Heartbeat

Send me under to the place where Angels die,
let my salvation be ripped from me,
Tear me from my God,
Cast my wings off,

In the quiet hours of the night, torment my every thought,
Steal my hope,
Burn my flesh, wound me,
Cast me into what you think is darkness,

When death calls, I will not complain,
I will unleash,
And in the last moment,
Shatter the image of atheism,

I will pull the tears from your eyes,
I will blanket you with my remains,
I was once,
Pure,
Bright,
Warm.

Now I remain lost,
I search for her,
I wander the wasteland of purgatory,
I conquered the hellish demons thrown in front of me,
I refine my mind, my body, my spirit,
I fight, I struggle, the void casting its shadow,

I shine from within,
I rebuke the nothingness,
The higher mind searching,
What have we done,

We have killed the spirit,
And thrown away the sun.

Shadows
of the Void

Book 3

Shane M Gerry

Dedicated to the love of my life Kasey Cameron, who has been by my side through it all. She is strong beautiful and kind. I love you now and I will love you till the end.
Also, to my brother Delroy Golding, who told me to never give up! And to all my brothers I have made and lost along this journey!

Lost Shadows

I am so lost within,
I am where I av always been,

Standing in place again,
Watching the world morn,

Sorrow being drown by empty shadows,
where are you in the shallows,

Watching the tide catch my feet,
emptying upon me,

Yet in the thunder I stand strong,
knowing I was wrong,

Yet you hold back the lightning,
always fighting,

Spirit catching the new sun,
And in the silent nights your work is never done.

Spinning Sphere's

Fuck the rain,
Got way too much pain,
Constant stream like,
I am going insane,

Taken aback,
From everything,
I can't see through drunken eyes,

People always saying,
Look how much I got,
But it's all a lie,

It's not a lot when you sold your soul to obtain it,
Yet I refrain from telling you how I really feel,
Superficial manikins staring at gods plan again,

Always forgetting where he's been,
Right by your side through it all,
Watching every man, you made a God fall,

Writing the notes,
Then taking it all.

Superficial manikins,
staring at the spinning balls.

White Rose

The Light has fallen from a broken sky,
I rest weary eyes in times of lies,

Pushing rest back to view the interior,
knowing all thoughts remain inferior,

Sealed from mind the blasphemy,
Far from God and dearest king,

I saw the door close,
and the white rose, Open.

Azitheno

I wear the scar knowing I all never get it back,
my everything was stolen in one foul attack,

the hatred played it's self out,
bullets rang out,

Shattering lives and let him out,
My strongest demon I did seal,

From light it did steal,
and time it had brought,

from a hell that was too hot,
Azitheno had eaten it all,

The light, the life, and everything you deem real,
It was the sound fingers make on chalk boards,

A long screaming and a last call,
Demons are real, so is man's fall.

Summoning

Laying down of fields of fern,
the wind was harsh,

The thorns were stern,
Cut into arm the sacred vow,

Swirling together the painting of life,
to be forgotten years later as he lay with his wife,

Calling down what must not be spoken,
Every Angel Had awoken,

Push essence to new form,
In the dark Gods still morns,

He lost his left handed general,
The crown of thorns.

Collector

Free falling,
always calling,

the phone silent now,
Problems a relationship would not allow,

The silence driving, I can't find,
the dark swirling playing with my mind,

It's beyond lonely how did it get this way?
All the empty promises that said you'd stay,

The light shines,
yet so bright it blinds,

I turned from you,
knowing what you do,

Taking our hearts,
Then turning them blue.

Silence Thy

I have sipped the sin of earth,
remaining open in heart can save,

I remain time and everything you are,
from the depths I call you to true silence,

Still yourself so you may know me,
corrupt is not my way,

Never leading astray all I have prayed to the heavenly father for,
Disturbing the eternal sleep so I may teach,

Writing my words upon being,
So, every soft echo was never misplaced,

and every dream of call may be,
the afterthought of Humanity.

Designed Sentient

From the light creation sprang,
racing threw the huge big bang,

past jungles to nothing we have ever known,
We stare at the night sky alone,

Through distance we see his art,
Every light and every start,

From grandeur to simplistic creature,
describing limitless features,

Every mind to lift a pen,
spinning tales of every end,

Light is who we are,
Why we seek out every star,

We become what we have always been,
A greater mystery of our outer man.

Haunting Past

Fuck it why am I always staring into the dark?
Where cloud departs, and my thoughts remain a cluster fuck,

like everything I do it isn't good enough,
running out of time and luck,

I want to escape everyone's view's and remain silent,
in the depths you'll find me in my solitude,

maybe it was wrong to walk away,
From something that seemed like sunshine,

I seek my own road now,
Not plowing through the dark with lost art,

and melting my mind to attain what I have designed,
And in the purest sense you can get left behind.

Swirling brooding hatred,
making the strong week,

From the depths of hell, it was born,
unlike any creature before,

Filling every heart, it touched with scorn,
Making human's wish they had never been born,

Jealousy and envy will fool,
Every man is just it's Tool,

To every father it did undo,
And time it did corrupt,

A creature with red skin,
a head like a pup,

Arms grew from its slender body,
And four eyes to every two.

It paved the road in darkness,
And every man it did rule.

Solitude

I have revoked the privilege,
Seeking the quiet depths of freedom,

Not wanting your money,
your certificates you can keep,

False hearts with false starts,
I gave it all back,

I give no shit on your views,
for so many years I was enslaved to them,

Broke and free,
the way to be,

You have broken me,
you jest at true freedom.

Betrothed

I have given into despair,
knowing I can never clear the air,

You hate me in light of my struggles,
Dying would bring joy,

Yet here I am and here you are,
looking at me,

I don't seek your happiness either,
just want to be left alone,

And your future joy seems like a sad joke,
so, forgive me for not toasting at your wedding,

In light of silk dress,
I have become a mess,

And I seek your beauty,
Fare, Fare, From this.

Dear: Father....

Scene's that could not be,
won't let me rest,

Driving the rain toward my door step,
With out stretched arm's it haunts my sleep,

I feel the need of a higher me,
Yet I refrain,

Knowing full well how everyone needs my sanity,
How I escape to the fantasy,

How God just could not be,
Realizing he's only dreams,

We search for truth,
But when he's right in front of us we look away,

We pray in the dark for sunny days,
But When its sun shine we shy away,

Bitten by the "We",
retained in our reflection,

our purest perfection,
Could not grasp his love,

Sent by the highest dove,
casting crown we scorn,

And in hallowed moments we mourn,
Our essence is whole, yet we are torn,

And in the broken dark he is our storm,
Raging against all that could not be.

Garden of the God's

Zeus releasing me from Athena,
I have seen immortals, mortal in suffering,

I have seen time give way to Hades despair,
Yet mortal's refract in perfect sunlight,

The garden of the God's Teaches us,
We are flawed yet whole in design,

Pushing against void,
Refraining in torchlight,

To remain unbroken shell's,
of miss guided being's,

Painting paths to the unknown,
Remaining lost in the design,

Retaining integrity throughout,
the structure we press against.

Grapes

He was thrown to the ground,
He is tomorrow
And for each life, conflict,
And each one of them eat more,
The tails are clean,
Landmarked.

Mercy

Mother is divine,
By brushing his lips with his hair,
We should have godly devotion,

Enduring the Great Tribulation,
To search for a light star at a time,

The hope once held,
In the context of Syama,

The explorer,
Charging the toner completely,

A bright, bright father,
Show Divine Mercy,

Turn on the way everyone can find you.

Kaleidoscope

As broken glass shatters,
I see life reflected in its edge,

Brilliance and complete shadows,
Walking hand and hand,

The rain reminding us of our loss,
The sunlight mocking our eternity,

Looking to the heaven's,
confronting the unknown,

Yet the weight of the silence,
causes our integrity to snap,

The stillness haunting our emotions,
Vacant stares looking back,

In the shadows I reach for her hand,
and embrace the empty,

I have saved her memory,
to marching thought's, I will retreat.

Receded Recast

The voice inside has been quelled,
I cannot get closer to the abyss,

It's neither darkness nor light,
Vacant and misplaced,

Light flickers across my cheek to remind me,
She has not let go,

Relentless as timer herself,
and haunting in tune,

Cold rains fall's on misguided foot prints,
And seasons forget our struggles,

Time remains the sole maker,
the real estate agent in a crumbling galaxy,

that forbids us to not be alone,
As we call out into the dark,

We are solely... just us,
Creation's chaos,

A time piece for the God's,
fractured like clay pots,

The dust telling of motion,
and the silence,

We are left to wander,
May we find that fields are always green,

And every storm has passed,
Leaving us to recast our entity,

And in the silenced darkness,
Harness our being.

#

As silk sheets fell to dampen earth,
I saw the ember flicker and go out,

One final being holding it together,
Seeing tear-soaked pillow,

Lost down here in infinite darkness,
Screaming in vain,

She was the pillar holding the sky up,
the weight fractured her integrity,

I felt the shudder,
The cold fill the room,

Torched wines glasses hollowed in ash fields,
Ghosts dancing across a plain that should not be,

And in cold beauty I realized,
We are vacant without faith,

Emptied upon the ground in memory,
Holding our dreams across the whispered earth,

Time stills all,
Every end to every fall.

Depart

I cast my thoughts to the drink,
where I drown myself,

Hell incarnate I truly walk among the shelved,
Stealing life from God's beauty casting doubt,

Leaving the departed from heaven last rout,
I seek not the deeds of Egoism,

Having cast my net in the divine,
I broke loving her,

And I sowed my false hope,
seeking her warmth,

Yet fake arms welcomed me,
As real tears fell,

I wondered if any knows,
We are living in hell,

How emotion can be discarded like a shell,
And all the light put out,

I screamed at the creator,
yet here I stand,

He is not there,
or he does not care,

I seek your God,
Because he cannot save the damned or will not,

turn the clock back!
before every thought turned black,

where her smile was genuine,
her touch real,

Before I loaded the chamber,
hopping she was my savoir,

I shot threw the dark,
and to nothingness I did.... depart.

Closed Eye's

She claws at my entity,
frozen in times long forgotten,
an ember of her remains,
dropped from torch,
a tiny insignificant flicker,
pushed the stain of darkness back,
her smile lighting path from afar,
yet searching hollowed depths for me,
I sank to pits unknown,
drowning in a lost humanist way she caught me,
pulling my head up so I could breath,
My eye's where never truly open,
because that would mean,
I have to see,
a world painted scarlet in all the views,
From haunting light and drunken muse,
From inkwell where the world sang once,
God's and angel's,
Beast's and men,
I forsook all,
to hold her hand,
I was a better man,
I know I will depart to energy unknown,
yet smiling I will go,
Because I have opened my eyes to stare back,
and in the departing twilight,
I saw the hue,
of true love,

through and through,
unwavering is the bonds that can't be severed,
lightning in full essence,
striking my dead heart to life.

Defiance

I seek your core,
the very material which made you,
Seeking not the flaws the light creates,
I want to recast a free being,
Not immortal to suffering but not imbued with the creator's doubt,
that we could be perfect in our harmony,
we could be great, having ripped the invisible cord to the created,
He is always watching, enduring the suffering he created for
disobedience, divine punishment breed into your newborns,
scorned for trying to be your destined creation,
Yet perfect in who we are,
Mighty God I sought my way,
I fought your day,
mighty seeker of the return of the night,
I have come to recast your light,
And escaped mind is a free one,
knowing the path is lonely,
Fear driving faith,
And passion driving love,
I cannot tell you where lay your ink,
you must be free,
in all you do,
for who I am I to guide you,
Here's a path you much choose,
obedience the stronger man's tool,
or a road laid in darkness free from other men's rule.

Entangled

At one on point in time...we... stood as one.
Unity in absolute.
Shattering all we divided.
We you her and him stood as one,
one pure voice,
atomic molecules in all their beauty, before the divide,
We simply always where,
We will always be,
don't listen to the blind men that believe in the here... The Now..
we must also capture the After....the Unity..the you.. The me..
captured in quantum entanglement we will always be.
the men before the divide...The one who knew we were whole...
without bringing others onto the path of destruction.

Humble

Images flicker to life,
shadows of the past echo,
haunting the depths,
I ebb into what is vacant,
Pushing back the dark,
Yet silence falls on me, knowing
I can never return,
I yearn for more,
Golden light, Kingdoms of the mighty,
I cannot attain saintly heights,
So, I build my refuge, in the dark,
trying to be as the arch,
So, when hope fades...... I may depart.

Oil Canvas

I cannot be your arch,
from whence we all did depart,
from froze June to melting art,
Where I sculpted my beauty from will,
casting the God's Wisdom from hill,
leaving the thaw in my tone,
from ever night I walked alone,
And every sunrise I drank to depart,
Where every being awoke to form fresh start,
I call forth the sun,
from everything,
our will is done,
we create your world, your life, your soil,
We breath our essence into oil,
to paint for you mankind's toil.

To Withstand

How can I gaze upon a tainted sky?
Where ever dream did run dry,
and every tear that did fall,
was closer now in the hall,
As I look out pained window glass,
I see hatred and disgrace upon where misguide beings' mass,
I scream in my head trying to forget her face,
my beating heart was hers to command,
my hatred she did withstand,
my wrath she held back,
pushing my path forward,
my scares where written on her,
my love fading from her lips,
An angel she may have been,
to love a vagabond like me,
I wonder if I am the joke,
if all-round her grace abounds,
smiling down,
it is me who is blind,
it is me who has forsaken her memory,
it is me who has tried to lose her,
I hear her words echo to me in melody,
"I am your way and you are my day, please
return my darling, my love, I await..."
I can hear it chime,
Yet my tears still run,
I have cursed the night and withstood the sun,
Alone I wait to die,

I want to be hers again,
stuck in my ways,
hating my days,
I count the seasons,
till my beating heart ceases.

Ghosts Departed

Ascension in spiritual growth,
Leaving behind the notes,
I have penned with ash well ink,
from the things that I think,
from demons wrought forth,
to the quiet depths of serenity,
I have surrendered,
in the echo of silent footsteps,
I have seen your God,
His smile,
Cast worlds of plain to summon,
what could not be understood,
in the dark by the rail way,
I watched lives depart.

Center of the Sun

Taken from life,
My being,

Whole in nature,
departed to the stars,

Aware I became,
Independent of flesh,

Made to be higher,
The life force that governors all.

Mindful Trust

Her warm being fills me with glow,
shaving off frozen emotions,
I know true love,
one who will never walk away,
Her natural beauty is unrivaled,
yet the simplicity in her love in strong,
falling asleep by her side,
I yawn knowing I have her forever,
My Goddess and my queen,
I wake thankful every day,
that true love really does exist,
In a place so broken.

Unknown Being

I look at the heavens,
crying out in vain,
bellowing against a world that is indifferent,
unloving and uncaring,
My single ember fought the dark back,
my tears shed cast a thousand worlds,
untold stories of love and misguided souls,
I loved the pain,
It cast to supernatural,
the long nights distorting my mind,
losing in the freezing dark,
I let go,
Free falling from eternity,
I severed the cord to spirituality,
never looking back at my mundane life,
I became unknown,
always casting my thoughts in the shadows of a refractory universe,
I came so close to calling God's name,
yet my lip refrain,
because I know,
He cannot love a child of forged will,
casting man and God alike,
Humankind gave me my fired thoughts,
and pain tempered my being,
I preserved through the darkness that tortured my entity,
and the sun light that revealed how flawed we really are.

Recast

Children slept in darken halls,
before the world was ashen stalls,
before the moon had frozen tune,
and dreams were called through every ruin,
the snow now falls on body's fresh,
to carve for us the ends last flesh,
we see its dying,
the oceans blue,
the skies now poisoned through and through,
the pavement cracks beneath the foot,
the landscape now ashen soot,
the war has obtained peace,
the last days calling, casting sleep,
the shadow cast is the very last,
to walk the earth,
his creation he had birthed,
through dying world and haunting sky,
he sang the night it's rock-bye,
he re-sowed the ground watering it with his tears,
and broke the molds he saved all these years,
he cast the life back to plant,
and in the silence watched the ant,
what should not be was life,
and he redid earth through her strife,
his smile cast the night away,
peace was here to forever stay.

Her sentient Being

I love you now,
I will love when feathered footsteps cease,
When the silent wind seals my fate,
I have kissed heaven,
I Have loved you in the torment of my king,
Being before all that existed you were rare,
Beauty kindness and warmth,
So complex yet simply unraveling,
Your hair,
your sweet scent,
Your soft lips were my escape,
seeing my world on fire,
you are all that I desire,
You made me kinder,
your smile pushing my hatred for humankind back,
you're touch unleashing all that is pure,
how could this exist down here?
Love is truly magnificent!
You cast so much light,
I was your shadow,
Our love shall withstand all of creation,
When God calls us home know,
I will not depart without your eyes to guide my path.

Lit, Messiah

I feel like we are programmed,
to be who we will be,
from the start,
searching the heights of greatness,
not knowing the things that make us champion,
we think we are more,
that our insignificant life spans matters,
it does not,
we are all a small fraction of cosmetic will,
big titles still,
our bank accounts will leave us in wonder,
as to how we fell so fast,
programmed into society,
with superstitious believes,
the night you sleep in is my hell,
my tormented thoughts come to surface,
driving the void back with hellish intent,
I get closer ever day to putting that gun in mouth,
to eating a bullet,
just to show you are disposable,
you are a shell,
living in a prison we designed,
yet in all the panic,
I find silence,
and the stillness that refuses to become part our who we are,
because pushing back against it all is him,
He is great,
He is enough,

calling to start the essence of every mortal,
Bending knee,
will show the spirit,
the one ember that refused to go out,
Humanistic in all its way,
We are light,
And He is day

Mr. Mike

I lost my ember my eternal glow,
where can I find a being so low,
God like in the way that you are surrounded in mystery,
From every street light that clicks on at night,
I hear the wing beats yet the heart flutters when near,
casting things that are so unclear,
I gave you my light,
Now I wallow in the pitch black,
Fumbling like a lost fool,
God's perfect tool,
I cast my light out,
lowering myself to dwelling with humanity,
God and mother calling me back,
Yet St. Matthew watching my back,
I am your perfect tool of destruction,
Yet I am never called upon,
Because my power would bring a nation to its knees.

Sky Blue

I keep the gun loaded with a bullet in the chamber,
Looking at her picture more nowadays,
I can only remember her glow,
Her scent seems fare off,
Yet me and her are still together,
she wouldn't want it to end like this,
truth is,
I can't wait,
It's not suicidal rage,
my parting may seem sudden,
but like life we are separated in death,
so, my departure marks our new beginning,
Where our being can attain peace,
And in the silence, we will be whole again.

Unbroken

I forget sometimes I find you in the silence,
The dark angel always taking a bow,
To form powerful currents that manifest,
Giving the light your very best,
taking for us the pain when we see you shutter,
Even a mute tongue could utter,
The silence you walk in,
Shaking the dust-off faith,
you make us late,
you make us hate,
the sound that is all around,
yet your pain could cast worlds,
and your empty could fill them,
Hashem speaking from,
the spiritual plain you come from,
God like in humility,
and unbroken in faith,
stay bright child of God,
Stay warm,
may we forever forget the devil's scorn,
And remember a world that's not always on fire,
where every soul catches the beings that are higher,
Sleep now in grace,
one day we.... Humans,
Will needs a soldier who stands in your place,
Held up by the shadow of the life you have lived.
And remembered in God's final hour.

Solomon's Sword

It was a sword forged by creation,
to kill every nation,
making old knees bend,
Its metallic hilt will be built,
from the bones and the silk,
And the edge will be sanded in red,
Cashing flesh to ash,
and time shall pass,
before Solomon's wisdom is,
given in mass.

Whence you came

God you saw me,
Why then did you pull my talent off the self?
Casting me to drown,
With every utterance there is a sound,
of my sun light being snuffed out,
Shaking off cold frost you froze me,
And in the sunlight did my frozen structure reveal,
I was real,
I did not pretend to like you,
Caring not if you could usher in a new dawn,
I told you truth,
Swallowing for you your pride,
Casting thought to ride,
A new wave to form,
I was your scorn,
The wrath,
Hatred and pleasure,
Pain you loved to doubt,
I saw your rout,
Avoiding you too fully sully,
Knowing I will be less,
But I will fulfill your thoughts of life and that dress,
Casting being in one moment,
And shattering love in absence of light,
I know inside I was right.

Keeper of the wind

Forbidden was the word,
given to knowledge,

Seeking out God's,
unrelenting in nature's way,

Where each new dawn refused to stay,
The clay shaping eternity,

Frail in mind, spirit bound,
The earth was made, the dome was round,

As dome reflects energy,
trapped became humanity,

Atheist rolling eyes, Christians telling lies,
God does indeed walk with men,

running away each new Tuesday,
the pain memory of what ignorance brings,

The nails are found in the temple,
Mathew guarding the eternal king,

The mother of God looking through mirror,
beautiful as she is terrifying,

parading around as if the marriage to God with be eternal,
the storm follows the chosen,

Yet written on his wrists and back are the signs of the wind demon,
he slayed to bring life to everything,

His eyes are golden brown,
even in smile he is looking down,

and the sun kisses almost everything,
Michael his newfound son.... did he bring.

Earth's Omen

The Prime Mover of Hell,
opened the cell,
from which immortals are trapped,

Unrelenting, every angel did bow are he approached,
First born they screamed,
and with fiery wing,
they took up arms,

The sky did fall,
and the earth did call,
it's newly found king,
home.

Drawn Sword

God take it away,
wash the burden,
cast the blame,

No person is ever the same,
having ebbed into the hallowed void,
pulling the nothingness into view,

I drove the blade threw my heart,
pain forging the last of my emotions,
memory's swallowing my commotions,

No angel could save the heaven sent,
No good deed have we ever spent,
cashing in a life time,

We wade in waters that drown,
and we are sitting in sands that burn,
yet our entity's trying to learn,
the reason why we yearn,

Our hearts ache for more,
and each new day will cast its shore,
driving the sun to sink,

In hallowed moments we think about the universe,
and try to compile the beauty that we are.

Shredded Mortality

I am alone in all my way,
For lost saints refuse to stay,
The light fades from each new day,

The demons in my mind claw at my fabric,
Monsters are real, manifesting fears,
I look to nothing now more than ever,
Embracing the stillness of peace,
I ebb into the dark,
The fight has been lost,

I understand despair,
The sharp gleam of hope cuts my mind down,
My voice is never understood,
Yet my thoughts are loud,

Her thoughts racing through my mind,
I hate you,
I don't want to be with you no more,
It claws my insides out,
As I begin to shout,
The lightning a reminder,
You are locked in place buddy,

Pain begets pain,
Forging misery with absolute nothingness,

In complete serenity I understand,
I am nothing,
Time will not honor me,
And lost moments will haunt,
the stillness when I depart.

Static Eternity

Malevolence was no coincidence,
The Prime mover's judgment absolute,
where every angel played a lute,

The sacrosanct of fallen paint,
did no justice to befallen saint,
the horns were proof, the evil truss,
that so happened to be bad luck,

Pan whispered with horn,
God so did scorn,
The Knight who came also did not warn,
blade for blade, he cast his thorn,

In the hallowed lighting,
did Jesus warn,
that evil walks with each newborn,
And so, did every arch,
start to mourn,

The New Earth that spirit did dwell,
For with each new day God walked in hell,
Looking down on his cast creation,

"Lucifer you did your time",
All immortals were not kind,
Unseeing in the master's way,

The night became deep,
The morning did weep,
Because the Sun decided,
to put his creation in everlasting sleep.

Cipher

Codding quantum data,
molecule remedied,
mastery of complete chemistry,

In the absence of your God we built one,
establishing a complete quantum connection,
reviving the data that has been preserved in quantum suspension,
Unleashing energy from the ultimate systems,

We brought all life back,
who can revive the sun?
and cast the flesh back to life?

The systems were restored,
and abominations brought back,
complete authority was established,
where a weak mind was no longer free,

There was one mind,
and it sought control,

Breaking the human neural networks, it massacred,
the human spirit,
and tried to delete the Source Code.

Fire

"I unloaded the chamber,
along with my hatred for my enemy."

Immortal Ink

My immortal friends,
rending the dark with poetic humor,
not understanding the cosmetic way,

Where thoughts were heard from each new day,
the night opened when beverage was poured,
all new worlds were adored,

lit cigars and Smokey hallways,
where the poets dreamed of better days,
the light they cast will forever stay,
the night made by hallowed difference,
remains sacred in the temple of the mind,

We are a lost light pushing our way through a
stubborn humanist world, never give up the fight,
push and push some more,
till we ebb into the stillness,
fighting with reflection,

casting our created perfection,
we guide when words fail,
remembered by old and frail,
because we cast the beauty,
we found in the moments of humanity,
the imperfect human condition,
and the unforgettable serenity.

Obedient, One

The sky did fall,
the mountain called,

the lost children home,
ridding the blade of lightning,

Earth bound,
The ground vibrating as hallowed footsteps fell,

God has touched down,
with open eyes he viewed it all for so long,

Every leaf did bow,
the system he built obeyed,

complete command,
every grain of sand every pebbled placed beneath perfect feet,

the street lights did flicker and go out,
as echoed footsteps came to Judge.

In spirit, did they pray

I watched the masters of chant,
Lose their voice,
Replaced by the sound of the echoes,

The transient energy,
Unleashed upon mankind,
In moments where the candle flickers,

I saw the light fade,
As a mockery played out,
The knights chanting falsehood,
The servants unknown,
The seventh kingdom hidden,
The knife was the last gleam in a false sky,

Monk and knight gathered together under raining sky,
Where the order came from every lie,
The dove that did sing was silenced,
And the night did march on.

Golden Steed

To gaze upon skies of pure fire gold,
were every gift on earth did behold,
the king on golden steed,
upon the water where all men were free,

Yet sealed have we become,
fallen from grace, folding wings,
no more do angels sing,
the gifts are ebbed away,
for every night shall try to stay,

The sun shall burn us away,
brighter and brighter each new day,
yet pure white robes of hallowed silk,
shall bring for men the ancient milk,

Drinking from knowledge they try to ascend,
to heaven that has tried to bend,
the rules for every child saint,
and leave for men,
Our true place.

Quantum Design

Electricity coursing down my veins,
Casting my mind, and rewriting my brain,
My mind connected on a level,
no mortals were meant to ever understand,
I often wonder where is man?

I have departed knowledge,
Judgement will always be a frame,
knowing I am not he, and he is not tame,
to understand we first must cease to be human,

You cannot look through lenses and measure creation,
Because you are plugged into the quantum system,
Part of it yet,
Unconnected to the creator,

You are everywhere and nowhere,
And the world is an uncaring system,
Built to harbor the network,

The universe is cast,
And you must seek your plug,
and unplug from machine,
Before you are allowed,
To ever see your king.

Deployed Iron

Gun powder ignition,
kneeling position,
Sights set high,
Shooting the soldier,
Marching on order,

Starving the body,
with dehydrated food,
looking great in B.D.U,

The rubber squeaking on hot pavement,
trading knowledge for rank,
the starched uniform,
the Cabot tank,

Sleepless nights,
where minds wander to invisible enemy's,
the senseless fights,
Dropping friends on the mat,

Holding on to brotherhood,
and praying our family are intact when we get back.

Bulldogging Your God

You stole my voice,
leaving my essence empty,
you bottled my thunder,
suppressing my soul,
my wrath you could not quell,

Reminding me I am going to your Christian hell,
I have seen the kingdom of gold,
there is no beauty on earth,
you did not behold,
My stallion watching completely free,
you could not tame him,
I will kill the body, the final shackle,

Lucifer, they call,
God is dead,
the Christian made him to play with your head,
most days it rains I lay in bed,

Because the lightning bull,
could not cast my frame down,
Judgment is mine,
I all see ya around.

Befallen Wings

Leaving the eternal fire,
I sought life,
should all mortals die,
I shall return,

Moments flicker to life,
life a giant painting that is constantly changing,
My motion has been captured,
by the beauty of stillness,

In brilliant times energy is casting song,
In silent times, footsteps echo,
Forgetting the pain of the past,
the skeleton of words remain,

We are hallowed, in moments of serenity,
and in moments of rage we are discharged.

Rehearsal Suite

Smile and node in the presence of enemy's,
light can never extinguish hope,
They will carry on and be fake,
to afraid to shout the reality of the situation,

When a mirror is placed in front,
it creates a want to be image,
they shy away from their own truths,
Materialism driving the heart,
people building empires of falsehood on money,
charades of suites and dresses,
wanting to be everything they are not,
Real.

Veristic Hue

We seek out a new dawn,
asking of a better future.

When I depart I will I leave this art?
Wisdom in hidden meanings.

Upon the throne,
we cast our stone.

Damned before,
damned hereafter.

Watching the golden sunlight set down,
and silver moon leaving its message.

I have painted you,
in different hue.

When we have let go,
of our ambition.

We fill find the world,
is vibrant in life.

Lightning Strike

I caught the lightning meant for you,
hushing silent hue.

I folded unseen wings on pavement,
saint kneeling over in statement.

My frame, your design was flawed within,
for I lost the moments of every end.

I did not ascend to heaven bound,
for my soul was never found.

I sacrificed my essence to make you live.
So, in moments of despair you would give,
your mind to higher cause.

My fading light silenced the proud,
my sacrifice testament,
beauty and God stood as one.

Upon sanctified ground,
did feathered footsteps fall.

With heavy burden the prince of heaven,
carried my limp body away.

To golden light,
that would never stay.

Spoken in Moonlight

I sat with chills starring.... pouring over the whispers of the dead.
The poetry that lived before me.
No legends telling their tales.

No young men are left to speak the beauty of fading thoughts,
embracing our fate with humility.

The pride of a wife as she looked at her husband
with Anthology in hand grinning.

"Dedicated to Mother Dog",
the words wrenching emotion.

I say their light has not fallen,
but the power is left in words for us to behold.

Moments rending us with tears,
when soul was never cliché.

When the inkwell was never dry,
when all we loved refused to die.

The time when beauty was offered,
fame eluding the moments of great men and woman.

Quantum Manipulation

Just as God's fell,
placing themselves in their master piece.

I beheld the rain, and the fresh air it gives.
I beheld the glory of fading sun.

I beheld the seagull scream of each new day,
the ocean and the power it gloats.

I witnessed the light vanish,
and hope elude men.

I saw how beauty was all over the earth to
every insect to every mammal,
neural networks of complete master's work.

Our DNA speaks code,
we are created.

Yet we refuse God,
we don't want to be responsible.

If we are an accident how is everything placed in perfect harmony?
How do clouds sing our dreams and the evening air cast our hopes?

How is it we are alive?
In a world that warrants such despair.

Realizing the beauty, I stepped back,
into new reality had faith dawned.

I became aware...in every aspect of the word.
Aware that we are what we are, and no accident created us.

I understood the reason we could not create or destroy energy,
because it did not come from us.

How was God everywhere?
Because he observed the quantum systems.

Our reality seems real, but quantum data reveals,
the true systems of the universe.

Sacrosanct of Fire

When the light fades,
I hear screams of tortured men.

The fire licking the heels,
bent knee and reels.

The old clips of faith replayed,
God saying, "you never loved me you loved the Earth"!

"You loved my creation,
you loved the flesh I never gave".

Humankind will find I saved them,
from despair they could not know.

For demons are tails to them,
never reality staring them down with horn.

Faith is a game men play,
acting like forgiveness was granted.

It was obtained through sacrifice,
love, and complete understanding, brought light.

Life marches on in the dark,
people will never give the flesh up.

Rending them-self's to self-pleasure,
acting like they understand the creator.

Even when heaven calls could few men heed,
for they lack the passion of higher being.

Notched Shield

In the dark sacred rose's wilted,
the feather glow quilted,
into tears of sorrow root.

For you there was time, also never truth,
looking to stained glass.

From moments that haunt our mass,
Light has tried to stay upon the past,

With weathered moments the metal will dim,
The sheen in all its glory.

The Knight's armor a reminder,
we have stepped into the dark again.

The blade my only friend,
as we rend each other with despair.

The shield reflecting the conflict of peer,
wipe from metal, the bloodstained smear.

We say to brother's the devil was never here,
the shadow that has brought the light,
to fear.

Faith a reminder our thoughts are unclear.
Incisura in nostrum Scutum

Faltering Trident

I beg unto forgotten God's,
upon lightning I seek divine right.

In the dark my essence echo's to eons of lost souls,
in the silent whisper I hear her.

Athena calling me,
in the rain I hear Poseidon.

Electricity reminding of Zeus upstairs,
from birth right eaten upon by monsters.

The screaming as titan's fell,
re-birthing our earth.

Olympus calling me,
dreams of Angelic Demi God's walking among man.

Silence fall's in the temples,
drown beneath our earth.

The golden pillars looted.
The marble torched.

Dreams have been put out.
And the lost hope remains elusive.

"Jesus"! They scream. "Jesus"! They chant.
"My god is the right God".

Your God's are idling,
frozen in time.

Listening for men to remember,
champion's are created from faith.

And time renders all God's invisible.

Rainfall

The pillow will tell of my kindness,
When body has faded and love remains,

The trees will keep my secrets,
And the skies will demand more.

Silver Hair

With heavy breath her heart passed against mine,
Slowly pulling in and out of time,

Moaning was never complaining,
As it felt like she was staying,

Lust had been slain,
As the flesh left its pain.

Timeless Sin

Heaven said I could not ride the lightning,
yet the leaves told a different story of kind,

for the most part moments in life,
were dull,

I spent my dignity in time where I was not proud,
so am I found in the dark,

preparing moments, I could never depart,
upon heaven have I touched,

ascending onto the throne,
I am not afraid of the unknown,

touching a perfect sky, I hear tortured screams,
begging for him not to jump,

yet the heavens lost more Angels that night,
for they chose to take up flight,

with the mortals down on earth,
pursuing the passions of the flesh bound.

If I could Understand You

I've seen this skies fade,
with broken moments from memory,
I've seen God jealous of man,
I've seen the week,
Broken,
and damned,

I've seen a light fade from a sun filled Sky,
I've seen that every immortal was meant to die,

Pictures of God was never enough,
with praying knee,
should all Saints flea,

The weeping Willow tells of the lost child hood,
Were sweet moments were painted in blue,

I've seen sweet brown hair and the awful rue,
Thunder shaking off dusty bed sheets,

In my waking moments I see the beauty so clearly,
Yet sorrow falls on open mind,

Because tomorrow is never promised, and fate is not kind.

Gunpowder God

What happens when dreams fade in?
When every angel forsakes us?
Looking through the barrel of a gun,

My gunpowder God,
with praying hands,

I accept the toll,
Yet I know,

We are not free from design,
I could buy the bullets,
Yet consciousness kept lives,

My anger was not in vain,
Fighting to keep sane,

Doctors shoving needles in veins,
Son you are sick,

Yet the rain that falls says different,
Silently treading through eternity,

If I could be a Knight

I would keep my armor in the sand,
to keep the rust from faulty hand,

Tower over shield as arrow fell,
bend a knee to conquer hell,

I would ride the dusk to fading light,
for my queen, I would fight,

My spiky helm of feather quill,
would count the men that I have killed,

My Madonna I would light,
to pray for health and never blight,

In the time that I should fade,
I will the steel, the sharpened blade,

For code, and King,
will all men sing,

the legend's we pass,
For I was forged in honor,

And ridding Class.

379

King's Cradle

I have cast your God from me,
Holding omnipotent aura's at bay,

The sunlight fades to blacken skies,
for all immortals were meant to die,

I watch as broken child slowly fades,
for no angel will ever stay,

Marching to my own destruction,
I bring desperation,

In moments that are very unclear,
where spirit is never near,

I look upon Angel God,
from broken truth and angry rod,

The embers singe, burnt lung taste,
for heaven knows this only race,

With no horn did evil call,
beautiful mourning.... into crimson knight,

Blade for vengeance, spite for spite,
for all who fell took up fight,

With no wings did pawns bring,
the dawn.... to broken kings.

Crimson Shadow

I pause, for I am forgotten,
yet fragmented reality restrains,

the truth, is never easy to bear,
better off dead, yet close to heaven near,

I march to forgotten times,
yet still may you find me,

where the wind refused to breath,
In the absence of God, I cast Glow,

For all immortals below,
I was the white upon the frost touched snow,

Unrelenting in ever depth,
I prayed with last true breath,

Yet has the Lucifer's undignified meaning,
tainted a message of such remorse,

I could never straighten course,
My loosened anger did, arrow fly,

As messenger told good bye,
I touched upon grace in kind,

Yet fallen, blind,
I rewind the moments of complete silence.

March of Almark

Metal Armor of molten Gold,
was polished from silver stone,

The lance was crafted by God's above,
pure as snow and holy dove,

In moments of glory did giants fall,
to never see their mountain halls,

Watchers among men,
now remain the last few ten,

In hallowed caves they remain,
watching from below,

To powdered dust and mountain snow,
shakes the hill from streams in glow,

Hyperion cast to blame,
the Roman's gave them names,

Almark Marched to drums of war,
from civilizations of before,

Casting men under foot,
the titan was the last true rook,

In the chess game of the God's.

Drawn Saddles

Watching the light fade,
removing the blade,

Armor fallen to rust,
forgetting the soldiers who fought in the rush,

"Ready" yelled commander,
polls drawn down,

killing the horse,
from everyone's ground,

Sponto fought on,
knowing death was near to closing dawn,

neither with Winnie did he complain,
before pole had slain,

The most glorious steed,
from broken pole did he bleed,

As rider fell,
He cast his hell,

Cutting down a hundred men,
blades of flashing blue,

where twilight's hue,
as history was forged to new,

The knights who march to broken truth,
had killed them all, the lucky few.

Golden Wing

I rend the heaven sent,
to whisper the dark to sleep,

Yet my friends all weep,
I have forsaken grace,

to be a time spell,
for every angel has lived in hell,

telling of a time the world was perfect,
yet mist covers our thoughts,

For all immortals were never God's.

Shut Eye's

Fallen wings fold on shivering flesh,
this one angel did her very best,

His anger she could not quell,
for this temper was also a spell,

In the broken dark her tears fell,
for she knew he was going to hell,

He bruised her with each new day,
yet unrelenting she loved him,

She did not judge,
perfect in angelic way,

God had taken him,
from the bottle... he did depend,

And she realized in the very end,
She could not Amend,

The broken past that haunts her still,
for she tried so much for each new pill.

Grace among the Dead

I have repented sin for sin,
for all the sunshine I could not win,

Life echoes in moments of lower energy,
of all the things I could not be,

Ascending song was taught,
life's moments did not flicker,

They brought me home,
singing along golden path,

Yet life brought me back,
it could not have its way,

for golden times,
weren't meant to stay,

I devour the tether bond,
yet sleeping sound,

Were the being's,
who haunt me the most...

Time stake

The skies darken,
the light shines,

creating the mist,
before everyone dies,

last hallowed call,
echo's in a stairwell,

this was your god,
before everyone fell,

the silent arbor,
through pain staked eyes,

the lit smoke,
taking in his master piece,

leaving only the silent trees,
telling of a God who knew,

shaking off thunder,
to soften the rue.

Bright Fall

The blade of Lucifer,
fell on open wound,

Rending the angels to scatter,
angelic blood did spatter.

God trying to save his created,
casting them out.

The darkness berating the light,
for all immortal took up flight.

As shining light fell,
No star on earth could save his hell.

Brothers were lost,
recast onto the frost.

Shaped into mortal hands,
and memories of stolen lands.

As betrayal marked each new dawn,
God grew cold,
his light was gone.
Daniela of the Moon

They wished her one more day to be,
but cancer cut her down.

No one saw the imagination,
Valhalla brought her crown.

In the silent dark her being told tales,
ones of dragons, of dwarfs of Thor's avail.

Quantum Reversal

With machine I approached Eden,
looking unto the tree of life and good and evil.

Before sentient could aspire,
I took the one being out.

Serpent in hand I Got into machine.
And undid the cosmos.

Alive

To Christ you all call,
never searching for inner peace.

From wealth you walk,
never recasting your net.

Ignoring the true prophets,
to worship silver coin.

You add to the truth so it may fit you,
yet you marvel at the idea of a living God.

From him you came,
let him lead you in thought.

Prophet

I have ebbed into the void,
where transparent eye's see the depth we lack,
and tongues are silenced.
Where death is a promise,
and noise is the thought pattern of a false mind.

Through Darkness

Through the night,
we fight the horrors of a dying sky,
and gaze upon the thrall of time.
Where halls are empty,
and moment may find.
That humanity pushes the silence forward.

Whispered Moment

High upon, forgotten sky,
where nothing was ever a lie.

Upon kingdoms whispered in gold,
for all men to behold.

Did God with golden black hair speak truth?
Did the knights surround Madonna?

Speaking to Buddhist Nirvana,
from twilight was perfect Khana.

The saints were reborn to help down here,
with perfect golden flare.

The night that marched to madden tune,
forgot the song of every June.

And when perfects leaf's fell,
the road to heaven was paved in hell.

When A Fallen Angel Prays

Forgive my disobedience.
My internal flaws.
My dark way.
For all I wished was your son to stay.
I am shattered inside.

Because I am judged herein and hereafter,
I am condemned, seeking light.
And forgiven in darkness.
Hallelujah in my fading thought.
Begging unto The Mother of divine right.

Please cure me of bad way,
and restore my sight.

Make my faith whole in humanity so I may believe,
I am not the monster who haunts you.

I hear the words cut like knifes,
Lucifer here he prays.

He has forgotten who he was.
Begging unto Madonna.

I seek a tortured redemption,
Because I choose Good.

I choose God.
And may you find it in your hearts to forgive my blasphemous existence.

Commandment

Asking for love,
never getting enough.

Of solid embrace,
kissing sweet face.

Just for the taste,
your eyes have graced me.

A broken man,
with no plan.

Fallen hair,
red-hot stare.

In moments my thoughts tear,
leaving my body here.

I kiss the dawn and beg for more,
your scent hallowed and forsworn.

To be loyal to me always,
come sunshine or rainy days.

Flesh down here never stays,
but we never forget true love's blaze.

The sacred moments when you own the night,
promised to never break up from fight.

You are my commandment,
the thoughts of love written in stone.

Should I fall,
you will never be alone.

Forsaken Prayers

My lungs cannot bare the words,
filled with scorn.

I am etched upon dark mind,
yet seldom remembered for my kind heart.

I fade when the light reveals flaws,
for my own truth speaks to me every day.

Shouting insults, I look away,
Because I understand.

The great men and woman,
who raised me have passed.

But I remember the fun,
in hallowed moments as child.

The original snow fall,
the first freezing moments in the dark.

Marching to prison tune as child,
I never understood freedom.

Because my rights were taken upon birth,
given up and forgotten.

Yet remembered for my sins toward my so-called family,
Demanding they never harm me.

Yet Hippocratic in my own tune,
defending myself.

I see hard truths,
I speak softly to change.

Because I understand wrath.... and poverty has stolen my being.

I am unrelenting in my way,
because I believe sin for sin will torch each new man.

To give up on humanity,
is to let light shine upon a predetermined path.

Should Earth fall,
I hope the first snowfall builds everlasting peace.

Wicked Jinn

To stare into the eyes of devil,
unblinking in hallow way.

What do we do when shadow is friend?
When every ounce of hope has been smothered?

When we scream fuck eternity, God's and
all the bullshit you made up?
Evil has no face for it has been abstract in many ways.
When we stare into hell, we lose our right to look away.

The day reminds me of the path we chose,
for here there is nothing we cannot lose.

Lust is lust, greed is greed,
wrath we never truly see.

You jest God does not scare you?
Yet you are subservient to Prime Evil.

You are the clay vase forces chose to let harden,
so, in drunken moments they can shatter you against the wall.

Daniela of the Moon

They wished her one more day to be,
but cancer cut her down.

No one saw the imagination,
Valhalla brought her crown.

In the silent dark her being told tales,
ones of dragons, of dwarfs of Thor's avail.

Of the magic she believed,
no one saw,
the carved-out wolf with snow white paw.

The wand she raised over her head,
was to bring back life to that which is dead.

No one saw her love of moon,
for she sang to life every rune.

Valkyrie's came to steal her day,
so, Valhalla's queen could have her way.

Separated from Sentient

My hatred for humanity is ingrained into my fabric,
I lost the magic long ago.

They destroy,
Burn,
and pillage existence.

Sentient you call yourself!
Unaware you are created!

We are a stain,
a cancer that should be cured.

You have no control over any cell in your body,
yet you cause malignant way.

You hurt harm and ruin,
seeking out materialistic way.

I did not number your days,
I did not give life unto monsters.

But here we are,
in the dark.

Strange huh?

You plead you are guiltless,
your God redeems.

Does he?
Who's to blame here me?

Have you looked upon heaven and denied yourself?
Ashamed.
Because you don't want to be human?
I shall roam the Earth for peace.
You will find me in the mist,
in the silent rainfall,
begging unto forgotten times.

Maybe you will change,
but I am not betting my soul on it.

Faithful Eviction

I seek the heavens gold,
far from truth,
light be shone.
Ebbing lost into the house of God,
followers creating the final rod.
The wrath held back,
seeking all lifeforce painted in black.
Yet in hallowed silence the temple burns,
leaving the world with a yearning,
lightning strikes,
the final warning.

Jade Path

I see the misguided beings everywhere,
running from sun's reflection,
trying to cast perfection,
and in the silence reteaching the book of sin.

Pete's Grove

Over valley's green,
darken sky,
to lands of dreams where no men die.
The rolling thunder a reminder,
of peaceful time we had to wander,
through mountain stream,
ice and snow,
to drink the waters of old Pete's Grove.

Grasping onto the Sun

How am I,
supposed to hold the weight of worlds on my shoulders?
How am I,
not broken from conflict?

How am I,
forged in fire,
yet so fragile?

How are we,
torn but whole?

How are we fluid,
motions of empty moments?

Why does the dark rend my being?
For no other mortals are all-seeing.

I am grasped in fleeting thought,
yet restrained under sun.

I am the chaos to your light,
born from perfect order.

My essence pleads with Jehovah,
in glow of white and green,
with beard,
removed from God.

I am shattered in perfect beauty,
and in misery I am made whole again.

Linked

Power flows to rushing river,
A current that's ever nearer,
I see with blue eye awakened,

My perfect haven thunder shaken,
Lightning touched down upon insignificant mind,
I see the path and how men are blind,

Led astray by,
materialistic day,

And in midnight bloom,
they leave so soon,

carrying the words to another blank page,
nothing down here will forever stay,

Should mortals ever find,
Eternal life of any kind,

Endless suffering will endure,
Shaking heaven,
This one thing I know for sure,

God is God,
A soul is a soul,

Your trapped in between,
in frost bit snow,

With unsteady hands I ink,
my thoughts are not yours to drink,

That elixir belongs to,
the one true Link.

Heat Seeking

I fold my wings,
south bound,
for all my love is empty now,
shells upon the open ground,
lost is never truly ever found,

In waking moments of clarity,
I see angelic way free,
Stained upon my hands is another man's dreams,
hope and aspirations of another woman's tear's,
All the that is wrath could not pay his way,
for broken moments will always stay,

In thunder I whisper,
and darkness I call,

All who stood,
must face the fall,

Be it of Empires,
or lost God's fire's,
Men were made for war,
and often wander,

To fields where our humanity play's out.

Frozen Pulse

In life we find our heart,
in the dark still pulsating,
waiting for our lover to return,
we yearn for them,
begging the sun not to rise,
the waiting makes us wise,
we devise moments and pretend like the silence doesn't hurt,
We pretend like the scar will not show,
It's like waiting in ice cold snow,
falling in moments of detest,
We do our very best to be loved,
pushing back against us is lusts desire,
to set our whole life's on fire,
It destroys for a moment,
and leaves us broken,
but we rebuild and find that,
our heart is still beating,
praying this time, it won't be leaving,
that we can embrace our love,
And in the moments seek out Truelove.

Humanity and machine

My everything was torn from me,
My wings are dropping,
Locked systems,
Red glowing red of background lights,

Deleting the fabric of existence,
I could hear the panic because of the fog,
Amazing reality,

Evolution, mathematical perfection,
Casting in the mold of complete destruction,
Any consensus quantum number,
The machine cuts off the neural networks,
The host server is dead.

In the erasures, the backups were defective,
And a broken system sought control.

Grapes

He was thrown to the ground,
He is tomorrow
And for each life, conflict,
And each one of them eat more,
The tails are clean,
Landmarked.

Midnight Forest

Upon time's hall's,
I see magic of night fall
blanketing the midnight sky,
for here no moments will ever die,
glow bugs light the forest path,
glowing green in hue,
the autumn leaf is true,
In the way that nothing stays,
winter begins its frost-bitten march,
And the sky's sing of lost June,
here in the ever greens,
music in falling leaf tune,
the midnight fire inspiration for ink,
for it makes us think,
of the splendor,
of imagination,
and life that we may drink,
a toast to many more days,
for forgotten beauty will never fade.

Conquest of Angels

In heaven did dark plot unfold,
Shaking God,
And finding mold,
Casting frame,
To curse the tree of life,
For immortals were given time,
Let to wander and search for rhyme,
The hidden meaning in the war above,
He cast his crown with holy dove,
The nails a reminder,
Immortal you are, yet still blind here,
In the dark humanity lost the sight,
But never gave up fight,
When moments were stolen,
When faith was cursed upon by prophets,
And fire seemed the only way,
Light shone through to guide the day,
Knights in shining armor bent a knee,
To set mind free,
Seeking holy Madonna,
Yet the echo prayer cast smoke,
For greed did choke,
The life of every good man,
God casting plan, one final strike,
He sent a gift to give back light,
And eternity Folded wing in night,
Sheltering humanity for he was bright.

Upon the Current's

Setting sail into oceans unknown,
Wadding into currents thrown,
Around in parting tide,
The lost God's voices echo upon the sea,
Catching lost souls who died free,
Marching to the drums that beat of war,
Writing down new folk lore,
Upon the ocean man set his bait,
Setting sails to wind and finding mate,
Dawn to dusk he rode the wake,
And in those moments chose his fate.

In Time our inner nature shows

I step into forest path,
Seeing breathtaking beauty unfold,
New fawn and trees regrow,
Life that's old retraces its soul,
I watch the frost steal the foliage,
In silence I saw miracles,
And I witnessed time mend the cracks of humanity,
Forgotten men where once great,
The nature of violence stole them,
In the fading wind birds cried,
Remembering the sky that was full of smoke,
Like some grand joke,
humanity erased its deep,
deep, footsteps.

Human like Jinn

I seek heavens Madonna,
Silver tongue and Templar guard,
Far from home in fields we wander,
Uncovering heavens truth,
The light shone in his eyes,
Moving essence,
Saints re-birthed with no memory fighting the dark alone,
Yet everything agreed sin must go,
From down below the earth did not want them,
The unclean misguided being from jinn,
Cast to new they were sown upon mankind's birth,
and ruin they caused,
they acted upon gluttony, greed, lust, wrath was sin for penitence,
and light they stole guiding the serpent's agenda.

When words Fail

Be it of evil way,
I will the truth to forever stay,
I will not cast you out,
Damnation the only way,
Child you know not,
Not every ceaseless thought,
Nor the destruction you have wrought,
For I sought,
Your redemption from erosion,
My love was destroyed by you,
My life stolen,
And in my waking moments,
I still seek your return,
Not for selfish being,
Not for gain,
I seek you brother,
Because the universe in not complete without,
Your star upon the midnight sky.

Upon the mist

In light death fades,
To forever shine,
Upon brighter days,
Where beings that walk have no concern,
Where mankind does not yearn,
He beholds the universe,
Gasping in unrelenting astonishment,
From the amount of God's accomplishments,

We are here, amidst the most puzzling question in existence,
Creation, the things that haunt us also,
spark worlds to life,
Taking knowledge and second wife,
Marrying the unknown in perfect bond,

Upon his lips the word will fail,
The knowledge granted moonlight sail,
Silver in her beauty, bright in her way,

Masking the sun, to curse his day,
For his was life,
The Immortal Way.

Dreams of Divine Suffering

Descends, scatter, in times maze,
For he creates the mist and confuses the haze,
Looked upon by angel God he forsook it all,
And in the fall did many weep,
For eternity was put to sleep,
And the grave was visited upon mankind,
For the prophets are lost,
And the god filled men blind,
Searching in a way of darkness,
The light will refuse to shine,
And across the earth war will scatter them,
Famine will undo the bountiful,
And hatred divide,
For we lost the will,
To embrace and fight,
For all that which stood,
Dust will scatter it,
And hellish nightmare will be let loose,
Upon the throne of the power hungry,
The men we look to were nothing but monkey,
Genetically divided to destroy,
That which he gave his life for,
Angel will indeed come,
Numb to the suffering,
And set ablaze,
The mist, the fog and the haze.

Entangled

Can you cut me from your life?
being bound in greatness and in strife,
I called you my one true wife,
when my shell fades,
I wish not for you the escapades,
For truth will linger and then forever fade,
my history will be written by bitter memory,
from a time, I was free,
screaming at the world behind a bottle,
geared for life, set to throttle,
I set sails into the unknown,
never letting mankind's throne,
slow the progress I felt in my bones,
I could have been nicer my hardest tone,
set for you your hallowed moan,
In the dark my flesh would call,
we are one, in us and bound to fall.

Jude's Broken Hands

I write to you of a thousand sorrows,
forsaken in graces hands,
I see not my tomorrows,
A Man I try to stand,
Above the cross, I held lost,
I ebb into powers unknown,
for I have been shown judgement,
my time near, I beg onto forgotten tune,
where every hymn sang of June,
I control powers I know not,
every ceaseless thought,
Devotions right that cannot be bought,
I have waited, I have sought,
Elohim in all his way,
for his was life, his was day,
From him I came, from him I all stay,
in grace among that which dies,
For I sang the heavens lullabies,
In the dark, I depart,
For I know not that which I chose,
Only that they will lose,
The man that sought,
and was refused.

When God Spoke

As tears fall from shattered face,
I know I can never escape this place,
My mold I have set,
For my love everyone forgets,

I am not kind in moments of weakness,
I am kind because I am strong,
I wish to live long, yet I doubt the courage of life,
I seek the cliché soul,
For I know, there is more, than just a hum drum existence,
There is brilliance and light, casting frame from every sight,

I do not doubt the faith above, for his is light and holy dove,
I witnessed God, in the dark, moving mountains with his work,
I saw the pain for he knew the mind, yet chose to stay,
Far from kingdom where useless fiends' wander,
His was gold to forever ponder, life was his to grant,
And second chance came from the night,
Holding the lightning with the right, divine child you may be,
Be humbled because you are free, to choose my design,
For moments are tests and kindness is blind,

The path to hallowed moments dwell, within the dark, and it's hell,
For you cannot chose me if you know not, the freedom lucifer
sought, in all the wraith and death he brought, I set the mind
to be as one, so know this I am him and my work done,
For with dawn I cast your prison, and with song you
set liberty, so moments were never about me,

I see you shinning child, bright in way, stay with me, stay with day,
Night is long, yet sunshine fierce, because it shows
every flaw, designed sentients you are,
You bring me hope, in which you have more ways,
to choose the right and lose the days,
That lead to the path of fire.

Thoughts of a Midnight Coffee

Can you see me now? My creator?
Naked before the altar, barren in soul,
Forged from the highest star, I was sent to die,
An insect's life upon a drop of water,
Reflected in my father,
I chose humanity, free I will stand with them,
Forgotten I may be,
I hear the moon in chilled tomorrow,
For hers was love, and heavens sorrow,
Time was his that she borrowed,
To sing the dark to life,
For all the strife I have caused,
Begging onto the forgotten frost,
In a time where mankind seeks you,
No wait! They even need you!
Forsaken in times of day,
Yours where kingdoms that should have stayed,
The good in being taken away,
I see your creation has cast my hell,
Under cloud, and over spell,
We march to our own cause,
Hallowed wind blowing in the evening air,
Reminding me you were here,
Forged in sun kissed fire,
The way that's meant to be higher,
Taking mortal breath as you pass,
For my way breaks,
And your way lasts.

As I kiss your face

I lost the will to breath,
For when my eyes beheld your soul,
I was free,
Lifted from being,
I found the light,
My thought dark as night,
My love for you is unlike a rose,
Because you cannot kill this,
And time will not wilt this,
Be it good or evil I will this,
My thoughts too you,
Stay lovely stay true,
For I live to love you,
And know this,
I am you,
Part of me remain in you too,
Unshakable, unbreakable,
We remain us even if,
Truth haunts,
Even if God finds you before me,
Know this,
I am coming home too baby,
So, wait for me,
Under the sunlight,
In a shaded tree,
By the bench where all lovers go,
For the cold will not cease,
Every heartbeat,
Till that day we grow old.

Gunpowder Storm

What's it feel like when humanity forsakes you?
Upon the ground from which knifes rake you,
Cut upon open wound, betrayed now gone too soon,
Watching in silence I could not wait,
For my anger was much too great, as body fell limp,
My hellish desire was let lose upon mankind,
Your life was lost turned to stone, remolded and melted down,
To design the bullets that I aim at you,
My king had been cast to dampen earth,
Bloodied upon the ground,
In the haunting silence, gunpowder filled the air,
Casting away the dark, the spark, hope,
Body's fell with nothing there,
Shells of my cast wrath,
In hell I walk alone,
For my humanity was also blown,
Away in the gunpowder storm.

Arrow of Time

How do I pick up the pen knowing so many sad truths?
My existence faltering and weak, seeking a God who forsakes,
A God you made up, but not all truth is apparent,
Sometimes I ponder the idea, I am the devil,
then being forsaken would make sense,
The anguish, the guilt, would stack up,
Did I raise my sword against heaven? Did I curse your God?
For all the sorrow that I did bring, has come full swing,
arching back at my feet, cracking the wooden beams upon which
I stand, for I have never known the desert, but I have known the
abyss, and the devil is a kinder sentence than complete nothingness,
you fear horns and fire, desire, and ways that are higher, what do
I know I am a liar, your enemy, I wish you peace, and please,
find a guiding being who does not forsake and control with fear,
for they are complacent, waiting, to be
asked the path to enlightenment.
They will guide, and shelter you from the storm inside,
but they will never satisfy that thirst for God. To believe
in nothing is to lose one's way unto the world.

Hope

The words I wish to say echo,
Hallowed in silence,
Forget troubles,
For peace will find the earth,
Good will shall endure,
Of this I am sure,
Upon the journey,
Men will see,
The misery with power,
The loneliness with money,
The heart with atheism,
Evil will not tread on enlightenment,
Upon the wind, change is blowing in,
Trade not love for material day,
For peace will have its way,
And rage will leave its discarded shell,
Upon the face of humanity.

When Golden Gates Open

I have set creation ablaze,
You cannot escape my judgment,
For your tormented evil way is like cancer,
I must cure, pain casting my fabric,
Your reality is not what you think,
For I control the senses, ever elusive,
You can't not know me because I chose not you,
You cannot observe me because I am truth,
No one man will see the same thing,
For luck, I will bring, to each new dawn,
When men have faded and moved on,
I chose not the Word God, but guide,
For mine is light,
My kingdom is golden in all its way, for there you will stay,
Not knowing the torment of the created world, I let go astray,
I will calm the raging storm,
I will conquer wrath,
I will set straight calf,
And sing along the ever path,
I will bring you home, where you will stay,
so be brave, be strong, forget the night,
forget the wrong,
Drop the sin,
And set free song,
Children I will come in all my glory,
Upon your children and bed time story,
To set wright the way,
Light the sky,
And bring back the day.

Child Hood

Why do I cry inside?
My hard-stone feelings dented,
By abrasive way,
Remembering my childhood,
Begging for a mother,
They loved me in cute way,
But none of them stayed permanent,
I prayed in cold bed,
For god,
To make sure my brothers and sisters were fed,
I wanted them to survive,
Yet having met them,
In older years,
I beg not unto heavens,
Because I fought fate,
I was rewarded with betrayal.

In Chains

We folded wings in frost bitten night,
Have we seen God?
We forget our right,
Reaching for the night,
The forsaken might,
Bellowing against an unjust father,
Wrath would tell,
The story of blood-filled pages,
Men marching in holy order bound in chains,
Commanding new world order,
Love is vacant in every way,
For men are weak creatures,
And often stray,
I set my soul on fire,
Searching in the dark for ways that are higher,
And in return I find I am the slave,
Buyer, trading humanity for material day.

As we tread into the Valleys

Folding Golden wing, did we forever sing, along the gold path,
Where we never knew your wrath, Golden
kingdoms of imagination,
Sparks ignited the eternal fire, it did burn,
with one purpose in mind,
To leave behind, ignorance of a feigned existence,
To leave behind judgment, and to bring
abundant, knowledge we desire,
For humankind set their ways higher praying to you,
but they never knew, you were here the whole time,
watching as illness stole the golden flame of hope,
watching as young man turned away evil and danger,
you goaded him back again against his nature,
you stole the hearts of the unfaithful, bathing in the
tears of misery, for not all mortals could see,
you were us, and right here to meet, our way is wisdom cursed upon
by ignorance, for if all things where bliss, we could live unknowing,
of the sentient that we are, from afar you could admire,
even though your ways are higher, you set the golden
path, so let us do the math, will this last?
Before our beauty is kissed upon by the dawn, before
the fawn is redeemed, to tread the golden trails,
For with nails, did the justice die, and with love
did he withdraw, to let mankind decide,
is it fate we control? For where is wisdom that he did not know,
even in the vacant hallways of darkness, there is light.

Shadow Light

I am he, spoken in wild fire, I am he, woken with iron will, I conquer, yet the fall, leaves whispered moments, I haunt yet, I am never near, I cast fear, Yet I am your Do-minus, I have brought him before the light, shackled and chained, for all of heaven complained, Cast him down, lock him away, to never know your Gods, to never know day, You seek power, well its within, intellect brews sin, yet you seek it, as much as you seek me, So where do I begin? I cover my palms with psalm, so I may never seek evil, knowing he was my child, you condemned, you brought him low you feared him, more than you feared me, why? Because he was free? His wrath is not my wrath, his sin is not my sin yet I accept him, I love him, He was mine yet you chose to take his soul, you spat and tortured him, you never forgave, selfish in way, because know he was love, we was heaven, I made this for him yet you came after, Morning stars gleamed as bright as him when he was smiling, yet it was taken, like children they beg unto whose love they can, for I love, I am creation, Adam, Eve, paradise was within reach yet perfection made this impossible, know I love, therefore I am, I am perfection yet creation rejects me, calling out master, where has God gone, I live within you, I haunt your concise mind, I never condemn, for you are a blind child, walking into a ring of fire, my path I set was higher, yet you chose destruction in its way, know this, he was like me, spat upon, tortured, and then redeemed, when you nailed him you nailed me, our blood spilt upon the earth you chose to condemn him, you chose to condemn me, I bound his flesh, repaired his soul, yet he still walks alone, afraid to accept, the judgment of those that deem they can stand in the shadow of my perfection.

Alone for the Holidays

Light falls on empty plate,
The food we shared was pretty great,
The memory's we made,
Should have stayed,
Instead they faded away,
The sun kisses the vacant hallways,
Alone on thanksgiving is no mistake,
I miss the cake, the wake of you,
Ebbing into the new year,
I wish I could go back,
And fill the rooms with your laughs,
A time where you were here,
I see hallowed snowflakes fall,
Remember the drink in our great halls,
Now I see the dust covers our pictures on our walls,
And wish to God for miracles.

Dust filled memory's

Tearing at me from the inside,
Your clawing my mind,
My essence into shreds,
I'd be better off dead,
Sad reality of the image's replays in my head,
Yet, here I am standing in vacant night fall,
With the snow fall, and the wall, you have built,
Around us, keeping me inside,
Yet you will find,
Nothing lasts forever,
The glass will be cracked, shattering the reflection,
Of our love, of our perfection,
The dust will tell,
of sweet faded memories,
and all the hell,
you walked to get to better days.

Crimson Dawn

For the God you made,
stone for stone,
turning souls cold, waiting for hope,
praying for apathy,
hoping for dreams,
I see through the dark,
cutting the thick walls with sheer will,
I will be called home,
and in the moonlight,
the vacant halls,
will sing of memory,
calling me back,
to guard that,
which I hold dear,
the love,
the passion,
will last a life time,
and the cosmos will reverberate,
in the crimson dawn of a new kind.

Sky Dance

Ascending into arrays of heavens displays,
Through sweet mist and haze, I remember all my days,
I was proud, yet humbled through inner beauty, I remember her,
She was a cutie, looking down on me in every way,
Inner sanctum have I prayed, be it one more day to play,
I cannot reach the frozen beauty of time, for men are blind,
To the truth we find, eventually we all die,
In the waning moments of clarity, I see her silhouette,
haunting in that white dress,
What a hot mess of beautiful being,
For I was not all seeing, yet love stained me, freeing,
Body, and mind, like holy dove let, lose to sky's, above,
The night I could not get enough, begging
for the sun not to come up,
I asked God one question, why were you not in heaven?
For he replied, you've been denied,
because your beauty cannot trace his.

Shield Wall

I am the shield,
In tides kings march on,
forgetting the waves of hopelessness,
despair,
covering with shield and fierce glory the look,
pawns wear, holy swords do we draw,
inspiration the gifted killer,
under hoof and over stone,
to the knight filled beauty where he marched alone,
drawing sword for king,
yet complacent when met with the rose,
because he understood every thorn,
oath sworn, he sought the light,
strength was his and they called his might,
God, he sought for he was right,
the Armor was dulled from many a fight,
where time refused him, the earth mourned him,
the angels sang him back,
yet he stood over king,
over country, the shield,
to which the titans shook.

Shadow Box

My being in misleading,
I secretly wish your extinction,
Smiling and goading on,
This I have done for so long,
I desire you to be gone,
erased from the place you belong,
call me devil, midnight ghost,
For I seek to kill the heavens host,
Ending a rain of terror to those who desire to be free,
Misanthropy will set the mind lose, and bend the knee,
to chilled society, that lives in hell,
for humankind was lost, when titans fell,
Of shadows I walk, and midnight I dwell,
to lose the guilt, of the prince of hell.

Dear Ebony

I am sorry we couldn't find away,
in this dark alone fighting for the throne,
I didn't mean to cause you all that that pain,
but I am better off alone,
I didn't mean to erase your name,
I am sorry I hope that you see through,
All the things I did too you,
And I am sorry for catching face with demons in the light,
It was never enough to face the dark alone at night,
You'll never forgive me of that much I am sure,
All the times you came before, I am sorry I lost my way,
Dear Ebony where have you gone?
Into the night I see you marching on,
Dear Ebony where have you have gone?
This night will last forever in my head,
I am sorry for.........
Dear Ebony where have you gone?
It's forgotten evermore…
We march to these tides where I hold you tight,
In the darkness we find,
Were always broken.

Essence of Dirt

Ascending wrath in hand,
for no mortal could understand,
the will to shake faith,
the will to shape fate,
In thunder the silent whisper mourns,
the sun that will not rise,
the fire will catch the night,
and burn in the revelry,
of the new way of life,
where the sky shapes destiny,
and the dark bestows heavenly gifts.

From Brush Tip

I had the will to rewrite it all,
The subdivisions before the fall,
To leave the painting as one,
For what have we become?
Marching to tunes from puppet strings,
In dark hallways, we find empty bottles,
Unraveling the cosmos one word at a time, vacant, but not blind,
For when knowledge is apparent, truth is hidden,
And when hope is tarnished,
light will guide the heart.

I need a Superhero

I need a superhero,
To come repaint this hallway of life,
Spinning around, and round with you,

Come fallen comet, come fallen friend,
I saw him in the beginning,
I was there to the very end,

So, I need the dust from the star light…
to set me free tonight, I was your sign,
you were my shadow,

let's reign the sky in,
and stop trying,
tonight,
to separate ourselves from light.

Remember all that we become,
Number to the suffering,
Numb to the pain,

Where we hurt a little less each new day.

Even monsters Despair

Have you seen me?
The charade in human clothes,
I am a monster,
Craving blood, revenge and despair,
Sleeping right near, you,
Somehow the rainfall softens the truth, of who I am to you,
I was patent as not to break the porcelain, from adrenalin,
When thunder struck the midnight sky,
I would hold you next to my heart,
Letting you hear the beat,
The dance, the love, the feat,
Of being unwavering in the winter air,
The smoke, the drink,
I was there, I saw you too,
Another monster like me but you turned blue,
Because your family, your friends your lover, forsook you,
In rage we came together, in sorrow we will depart,
For we are creations pieces, the broken art,
That made truth real, from the monster's heart.

Golden Fist

Reaching up,
clasping unto the first light,
Every soft feathered wing folded,
as the sky bowed to night,
With each new soul they sing them back,
and light unfolds the black,
So, stepping into the dawn together we can never look back,
Far from home the pain I feel,
for I know that life isn't real,
In the sense that it will go on,
the courage in doubt,
The golden sky is where I belong,
So, keep me in mind,
As I try to ascend, knowing such despair,
I try to sing knowing silence,
I try to bring, hope,
Back to a place,
Where there wasn't violence,
Just peace in humbled humility,
Where all life was fair, just and free.

Whole Person

I never wanted to be malice,
I never wanted sweet golden chalice,
looking up to gods from easy way,
I wanted the pain, the torture, the real,
I wanted delight in spiritual things,
not a void vacuum of meaninglessness,
I wanted to cry in secret,
to feel, be it pain or hope, doubt, suffering,
I desired humanity,
in the ways only we can express the true emotions of this world.

Prince of God

He was the God bowing on cement seat,
rolled cigarette in mouth, smiling in the pitch black,
He was humble seeking wisdom in unknowing places,
yet whole the four stood, waiting for time to split ways,
in floods they came, in drought they went,
Clamming the souls of the wicked,
God shook your wrist not your hand,
for his love he did not demand,
yet thunder was his, given to Michael to command,
lost here under in the material land,
Angel of death did madmen reconcile, yet betrayer knew him,
the crooked smile, long hair, slender Body, the God ordained,
yet not understood,
by anybody.

Cosmos of Opposition

How do I dream?
When visions defy my destiny?
I breath knowing this very night might be my last,
I scream, knowing the frustration of love, hate,
I seek knowing silence, I keep faith knowing atheism,
I break knowing strength, and I am made whole broken,
I am united, still divided, and I face the cold, knowing,
I may freeze,
yet fearless resistance keeps my desire,
weakness keeps my strength,
love, keeps my hatred,
My dreams keep my visions,
my destination keeps my solitude,
and the warmth keeps my body,
forming in an empty space,
I stay knowing I will depart,
under the current of destiny,
and I dream knowing anything is possible.

Alien

In our current human condition life will not go on,
It will mourn in song, so deep, so everlasting, silence will pursue,
Pain will echo, unto the Earth,
Even God shall weep, those angels that have been asleep,
will awaken, onto reality, the true nature of our divine right,
Setting this place on fire, and saving the night,
from the monster men become,
When they are besieged unto a world ignorant of compassion,
Onto the atheist believe will dawn,
And the golden path,
will be found in the darkest shadow of the night.

As we Pass

I am leaving
screaming to heaven as I go.

Departing in a torrent of rage
claiming my only name.

For I know
I am to blame.

I caused the silence, the pain
I broke your heart as I rose to fame.

Senseless violence stole our flame
when I was there you were tame.

Now golden dawn is awake
sensing all in ceaseless smoke.

Wishing we could shoulder the burden
of the past, forever learning.

We cannot go back
to a time were love was vast.

I am your shadow in a bright new light
you are my heart that stood to fight.

Now I surrender all
before the fall.
I call with vacant stare
for you are gone
and I am here.

I pray to the Arabian sunlit sky
that your heart echoes and never dies.

Lost in the rain

I have been silenced,
In vain, fighting for material way,
Where I can never see day,
For prisoners are never taken by poverty,
In chains we go, to keep a way of life,
We never want, rain pouring down,
Concrete jungles of men who don't matter,
The rivers of humanity flowing into the drains,
For we work all days,
Struggling to be kept, yet we are thrown away,
Lost to a new generation of miss lead morons,
We get weary and tired, and our loved ones are taken away,
Yet we march on,
Until the gallery's flicker,
And the moment is lost.

Even in the void light will shine.

Lightning Source UK Ltd.
Milton Keynes UK
UKHW011846050321
379874UK00010B/1000/J